THE COMPLETE BOOK
OF
TRADITIONAL
KNITTING

THE COMPLETE BOOK
OF
TRADITIONAL
KNITTING

Rae Compton

B.T. BATSFORD LTD. LONDON

First published 1983
Reprinted 1983

ISBN 0 7134 3460 0

Filmset by Servis Filmsetting Ltd, Manchester
and printed in Great Britain by
The Anchor Press Ltd, Tiptree, Essex
for the publishers
B.T. Batsford Ltd
4 Fitzhardinge Street
London W1H OAH

HALF-TITLE PAGE
Fred Walkington coxswain of
Bridlington lifeboat, wearing a
gansey knitted in the traditional
way by his wife and showing his
initials worked into the plain area
below the main pattern.
F. Walkington

FRONTISPIECE: Polperro fishermen
photographed by Lewis Harding in
about 1860, when gansey knitting in
this village was at its height. *Royal
Institute of Cornwall*

Drawing of a Swedish knitter by H.
Hocket, 1859. *Nordiska Museet,
Stockholm*

Contents

Acknowledgement

Without information, help and encouragement there would have been no book and I owe a great deal of thanks to many people, not least to James Templeton and Son Ltd of Ayr, Scotland, who supplied all the yarn for stitch samples and garments, with the exception of the Icelandic Lopi yarn supplied by Scotnord Ltd of Crieff, Perthshire, Scotland.

In particular I would like to thank those who gave so much more than the answer to a simple question: Mariann Ploug, Arhus, Denmark; Birgit Schutt, Nykøbing, Denmark; Britta Johanssen, Halmstad, Sweden; Jos Blom, Veenendal, Holland; Mr Blitz, Neveda Wollspinnerij, Veenendal, Holland; Jenny Schneider, National Swiss Museum, Zurich; Aagot Noss and Gunvor Schønning, Oslo; James and Margaret Snowden, Nottingham; and my friends in Shetland, Mrs Thompson, Mrs Nicol, Mrs Robertson, Mrs Bray and Mrs Shearer of Lerwick and Mrs Peterson and her sister of Unst.

I would also like to thank the staff of the Scunthorpe branch of the Humberside Library Service and the staff of the following museums, libraries and picture libraries: The Scottish Fisheries Museum, Anstruther; Rijkmuseum voor Volkskunde, Arnhem; The American Museum in Britain, Bath; The Museum of Costume, Bath; Historisches Museum, Berne; The National Swiss Library, Berne; The Costume Museum, Castle Howard; The Textile and Ethnographic departments of Nationalmuseet, Copenhagen; Kunstindustrimuseet, Copenhagen; The Irish Tourist Board, Dublin and London; The National Museum, Dublin; The National Museum of Antiquities of Scotland, Edinburgh; The National Scottish Library, Edinburgh; The Royal Scottish Museum, Edinburgh; Dalarna Museum, Falun; Rohsska Museum, Gothenburg; Tiroler Volkskunstmuseum, Innsbruck; Textilmuseum, Krefeld; Shetland County Museum and Library, Lerwick; The BBC Hulton Picture Library, London; The British Museum, London; The Mansell Collection, London; The Museum of Mankind, London; The Horniman Museum, London; The Victoria and Albert Museum, London; Staatliche Graphische Sammlung, Munich; The Castle Museum, Nottingham; Museet Falsters Minder, Nykøbing; Ethnographical Museum, Oslo; Kunstindustrimuseum, Oslo; Norsk Folkemuseum, Oslo; Le Bibliothèque Fournay, Paris; Le Bibliothèque Nationale, Paris; Ethnographical Museum, Stockholm; Nordiska Museet, Stockholm; Le Musée de Bonneterie, Troyes; Osterreichisches Museum fur Volskunde, Vienna; National Swiss Museum, Zurich.

1 Introduction

– I always was a knitter? Yes,
It comes like nature to my hand,
And that we rarely do amiss
Which we completely understand.
MARY HOW.   1865

As an introduction to traditional knitting, these words of Mary How's, already over a hundred years old, seem to hold the essence of why this book was written. It is the complete understanding of the various traditions which makes for the beauty and strength of traditional knitting. Too often a fashion design is less than perfect because technique, type of yarn and stitch pattern are at odds with each other. They have not evolved side by side, each adding to the potential of the other, to make a perfect whole. In traditional knitting only the best lives on; the awkward movement, the difficult technique, are discarded for a more fluent method, a more perfect texture.

This book has been written for all knitters, beginners and experts alike, who are prepared to learn more, to reach out towards a greater understanding. It is for all who have found the fascination of creating pattern and texture, stitch by stitch, row upon row, and who are prepared to admit that there is always more still to learn.

The enthusiasm of knitters from Tibet to Peru, from Iceland to the islands of Greece, has helped to create the book. Even when language formed a barrier, they were prepared to pick up their needles and yarn and communicate directly through the stitches themselves.

In remote homes on windswept islands or in isolated fishing villages, high in a mountain chalet or in a cottage deep in a timbered valley, even in a castle cellar turned workroom and a storeroom high above a folk museum, lights have burned, often long into the night, as age-old methods have been recalled, patterns knitted at a grandmother's knee have been reworked, and yellowed wrappings laid aside to show, with loving hands, a treasured item made by great-grandmother.

There have been others who have become as involved, as interested and as inspired by enthusiasm, without whom not one word would have reached the page. Jimmy, born and bred in Lerwick, never having been to the northern island of Unst, calmly drove off into the morning sun with no prior warning, taking unknown ferry crossings in his stride, to find a welcome in this Shetland new to him, though old in the song sung by the spinning wheel and the knitting that was discussed as the peat burned low in the hearth. My husband, with lens and film, tackled the task of bringing stitches to life in photographs; Jock downed tools to model, and Vivienne, having modelled, returned to graph paper and ink to create stitches in chart form.

For the few, a very few, who cling to the knowledge they have learnt from other craftsmen but are unprepared to share in their turn, I am sorry. From sharing comes contact with others, the exchange of ideas, the inspiration

PREVIOUS PAGE
1 The Old Knitter. Mary How.
Mansell Collection, London

for new patterns, an unthought of technique to be tried, adapted and perhaps adopted. My days would have been dull if the books which led me towards knitting had not been written, and so I have written one more book in the hope that it may bring some pleasure to others.

To make the most of this book, there are one or two basic principles which should be followed.

LEARNING
Whenever possible use the type of stitch for the method of knitting for which it was traditionally used. Coloured work is nearly always easier if knitted round on sets of needles, or, if there are sufficient stitches, on a circular needle. In traditional knitting yarns were never carried loosely over a vast number of stitches. Take time to look at the two methods of using colour and use the one that seems correct. When a pattern, coloured or otherwise, seems to be too difficult to manage it is invariably because the pattern has been divorced from its original technique.

CHARTS
For maximum use, and so that they may be seen easily, the charts for coloured work have only used symbols for more than one colour where it was thought to be essential. In all cases the stitches and rows necessary for one repeat have been marked, although in many charts the area shown is larger, giving a clearer picture of the finished effect.

For knitting round read charts from right to left on every row. If using two needles read the first row or right-side rows from the right to left and the second or wrong-side rows from left to right. Most charts can be used for either round or flat knitting, and can be worked in colours of your own choosing.

ABBREVIATIONS
Basic abbreviations used throughout the instructions are shown in the following list. Any special abbreviations which apply to a particular pattern are stated at the beginning of the pattern concerned. Round brackets () enclose measurements or stitches to be worked for different sizes with the smallest outside the bracket and the others, increasing in size, enclosed in the bracket.

Square brackets [ ] are used to group together stitches which, if they are to be repeated, will have the number of repeats required printed after the second bracket.

alt	alternately
beg	begin(ning)
cm	centimetre(s)
CN	cable needle

cont	continue
dec	decrease
foll	following
g	gram(s)
in	inch(es)
inc	increase
K	knit
Kb	knit through back of loop
M1	make 1 st by lifting thread before next st and knitting it through back of loop
m	metre
mm	millimetre(s)
patt	pattern
P	purl
Pb	purl through back of loop
psso	pass slipped st over
rem	remain(ing)
rep	repeat(ing)
SK2togP	sl 1, K2 tog, psso
SKP	sl 1, K1, psso
sl	slip
st(s)	stitch(es)
st st	stocking stitch
tbl	through back of loop(s)
tog	together
Tw2R	twist 2 right by passing needle in front of 1st st, K 2nd st but do not withdraw left needle, K 1st st and withdraw left needle from both sts
Tw2L	twist 2 left by passing needle behind 1st st, K 2nd st but do not withdraw left needle, K 1st st and withdraw left needle from both sts
yb	yarn back
yf	yarn forward
yon	yarn over needle
y2on	yarn twice over needle
y4on	yarn 4 times over needle

2 The Root of the Matter

2 Costume in knotless netting from New Guinea. *Ethnographic Museum, Copenhagen*

The story of the spread of knitting from the East is as fascinating as it is difficult to trace, with tantalizing glimpses of verified fact obscured by often repeated assumptions made without foundation. It is not enough to glance at early drawings or stone sculptures and claim that every texture not obviously woven must be knitted. Many countries, including Egypt, South America and Scandinavia had little need to invent knitting, for they had other textile techniques which produced adequate covering and made use of wool from the native flocks.

Knitting is not laid away in safe keeping as are rich embroideries and costly tapestries; it is often used, discarded when worn out, and therefore difficult to find when it comes to tracing its history. There is also the added difficulty of distinguishing true knitting, knitting as it is known today, from other techniques producing similar stitches. These techniques can confuse even textile experts, who, although knowledgeable in weaving or lace-making, may know little of the actual construction or subtle differences between fabrics looking like knitting and knitting which has been worked with a continuous length of yarn and needles which are pointed at one or both ends.

MISLEADING FACTORS
The fabrics made by four techniques are often confused with knitting. They are:
1 Stitches made with a single needle
2 Knotless netting
3 Sprang
4 Embroidery

Needle-Made Stitches
Amongst early items once classed as knitted are sandal socks worked in a twisted stocking stitch and thought to have been made by the Copts. Mary Thomas, in her *Knitting Book*, described the stitch used for these socks, thus making it seem likely that they were knitted. She also thought that they were made on hooked needles, such as are used in the south of France. However, Margrethe Hald of Denmark, and Dorothy Burnett of the Royal Ontario Museum demonstrated a method of making this very unyielding fabric by working with a single needle.

Also called Egyptian plaiting, the twisted stitch could be classed more as a form of netting, but with very close stitches which can only be worked with short lengths of yarn as the needle and thread must be drawn through the stitch.

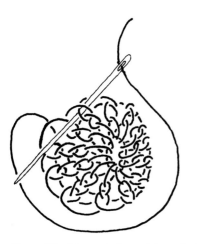

Fig. 1 Working stitches with a single needle

Knotless Netting

Knotless netting might also be classed as single-needle knitting but is separated here because of the difference in fabric produced. Used until recently in Scandinavia, found in countries as far apart as Norway and New Guinea, where it is used in making native costumes, it usually seems more complex in its coiling (before it is held in place by drawing the needle through) than the stitches used for the Coptic socks.

In Scandinavia it is known as *Nålbindning* or *Sömning*, in Denmark as *Knudeløst* net, in Germany as *Schlingentechnik* and is even found in Baghdad. Worked in wool it makes a warm, thick and durable fabric, which can be seen in a pair of mittens in Chapter 7 (*page 83*).

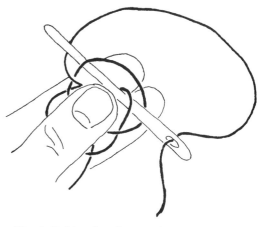

Fig. 2 Making knotless netting

Sprang

There are several different ways of working sprang but basically it is like weaving without the horizontal weft threads, their place being taken by the sideways movement of the vertical threads. It is worked by winding a long length of yarn over fixed rods or a frame. These strands are then lifted sideways over each other and are kept in their new position by the insertion of a holding stick or rod. The twist that has been formed above the rod is reflected at the opposite end of the frame in reverse. As row upon row of twists are made, the rod works towards the centre where it will finish between the twists made in the top section and the twists repeated by themselves in the bottom section. To complete, a thread must replace the withdrawn rod, otherwise the strands will simply uncross themselves. The centre thread can be seen easily in the patterned panel (*3*), and is often a clue to the identity of the technique. Where the top and bottom section are separated by cutting and used as two pieces of fabric, the line will be missing, but will have to have the threads held by a substitute method, such as a knotted fringe. Taken in a loop sideways with the under strand also drawn through in a loop it makes a twist even more like a knit stitch.

3 Patterned sprang. *National Museum of Switzerland, Zurich*

Sprang was widely used and over an immense stretch of years, the earliest examples having been found in Denmark and Norway, preserved in peat bogs, and dating from between 1500 and 1100 BC. Examples have also been found in more recent times in Peru, Mexico, Syria, Persia, Tunisia, eastern Europe and in York in England, although there is no evidence to support the belief that it was a technique worked in any part of Britain. The Indians used it to make pyjama cords, the Winnebago Indians of Wisconsin have used it to make woollen scarves, in Czechoslovakia it has been used for shopping bags, and in

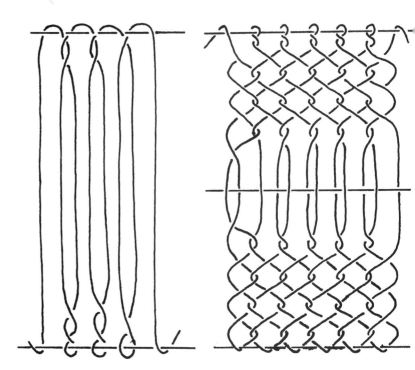

Fig. 3 First twists in making
sprang Fig. 4 Sprang almost
complete

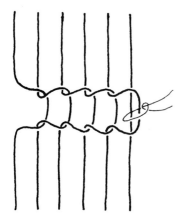

Fig. 5 A sprang movement to the side
makes a stitch very like knitting

the nineteenth century in Denmark, France and Germany
for making military sashes.

Embroidery

Stitches embroidered over woven threads can look exactly
like closely knitted stitches. Much the same effect was
created by the pre-Columbian Peruvians, working about
the same time as the Copts, producing fine and often
three-dimensional fabric wrongly called knitting. It was
worked in one of two ways on fine net which was
completely covered by the closely packed stitches. For
want of a better phrase, and without realizing the word
'knitting' would be misinterpreted, the textile technique
was called 'needle knitting' by Raoul d'Harcourt in
Ancient Textiles of Peru and Their Techniques. This he
regretted in a later edition when he realized the confusion
other writers were causing by lifting the phrase out of
context, a confusion which had never been in his own
mind. Before the arrival of the Spanish there was no
knitting in Peru although local textile techniques were
second to none.

4 The appearance of knitting achieved with embroidery stitches

FRAME KNITTING

Knitting was also worked in Europe on either round or peg frames but in this case the stitches are formed in a similar way to hand knitting and although given this assistance in support it is worked with a continuous thread and is correctly a true form of knitting, although formed without needles.

EARLY KNITTING

Having looked briefly at what has, and still does, cause confusion in the identification of knitting, it is also interesting to see what the origins of traditional knitting are and, as far as can be determined, how it achieved its present form.

Attributed to the Arabian nomads, knitting is thought to have been carried to Egypt, then by the Moors from there to Spain. There are, however, still items from India under discussion which may have been knitted before the eleventh century, and two bone needles found in the south of France, dating from the second century, raise the question of what they were for if not for knitting. The high level of skill reached by the Arabs is evident in the patterned silk cushions found in tombs at Burgos in Castille. These were made before the mid-thirteenth century for it is known that Fernando de la Cerda died in 1275 and his head was laid to rest on the oldest of the cushions found. Worked in violet, gold and white silk, in geometric shapes with eagles and flowers, it is not a beginner's piece and can only be the outcome of a craft practised over many years.

Liturgical gloves, also knitted in coloured silk, often decorated with gilt thread, are recorded from at least the eleventh century; there are also many gloves mentioned before this date, from as early as the sixth century, but with no indication of whether or not they were knitted.

SOUTHERN EUROPE

From about 1400 in southern Europe the influence of church requirements is found in knitted silk bags or purses for holding relics which carried small patterns such as those shown in figs. 6 and 7. Worked in many colours of silk, the patterns would be as useful today as they were evidently found to be over 500 years ago.

Fig. 6 Chart of a fourteenth-century pattern

Fig. 7 Chart of a fourteenth-century pattern

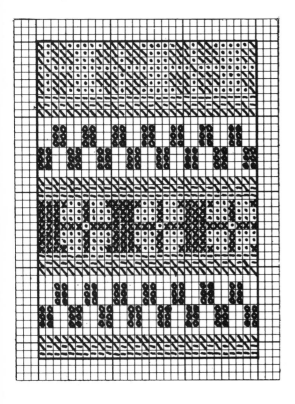

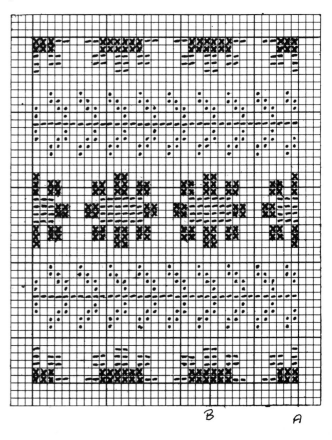

UPPSALA CATHEDRAL TREASURY

In the Treasury of Uppsala Cathedral in Sweden there is a glove which shows a silk pattern, still ornamented with gilt in simulated rings round fingers and thumb, and which may well be German because it belonged to a warship captain, Sten Svantesson Sture, killed in battle with the Danes in 1565. The glove was probably a favour from his German fiancée because the words 'Freuchen Sofia' are knitted into the pattern, which is worked in yellow, brown-green and orange or terracota on a soft biscuit-coloured background.

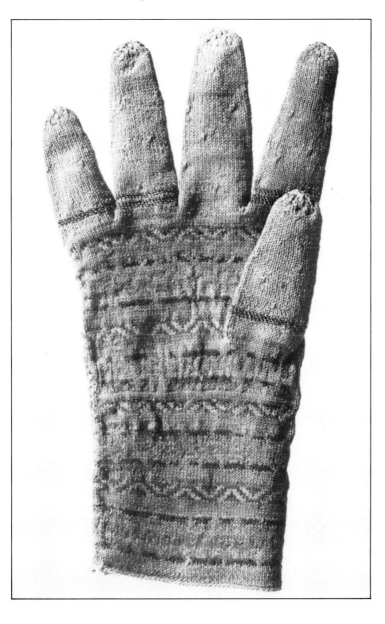

5 Sixteenth-century patterned silk glove. *Uppsala Cathedral Treasury*

MEDIEVAL GUILDS

By the fifteenth and sixteenth centuries knitting had spread throughout most of Europe, although not to Scandinavia, and gradually Guilds were set up to organize and control the growing commercial potential of knitting, now a craft for men to earn their living by.

The dates of the setting up of the Guilds vary. Tournai (1429) was followed by Barcelona in 1496, Paris in 1527 and the English Guilds later the same century, while Vienna did not obtain its statutes until 1609, later than Dresden, the Tirol and Prague.

One of the earliest dates for the Receipt of Cause, as the initial papers of a Guild are known in Scotland, is 1485, when the Bonnetmakers were established in Dundee. To be in a state where organization, rules, conditions and laws are required shows a fair degree of advancement and the actual technique of knitting must have been known many years earlier than this. The same, of course, must have been the case in Tournai and it is commonly understood that there was knitting in France before Scotland. It is interesting that Theodore Netto, writing one of the earliest books of designs for patterned knitting almost 200 years ago in Liepzig, states that the English maintain they learnt from the Spanish, while the French know that they learnt from the Scots. This belief is endorsed by Legrand writing in Paris in 1802, who claimed that the French knew the Scots to be their masters.

The Guilds were closely linked with the church and had their own patron saints, Paris adopting St Fiacre, said to be the son of a Scottish King; Dundee chose to have St Bride, the Irish connection being a complete mystery, for in other regions of Scotland St Mark was the patron.

In England knitting was sufficiently well established by 1488 to require the passing of an Act of Parliament controlling the price of knitted caps.

TOP TO TOE

Although knitting seems to have begun with coverings for the head, bonnets, caps, and hoods like this cap of 1562 made in England (6), stockings later became one of the main items made by hand knitters in large quantities, both for sale at home and for export. Even as late as the nineteenth century, in more remote areas, hand knitting was often supplementing meagre incomes.

MASTERPIECES

The introduction of coloured knitting to Britain is not easy to date whereas in areas such as Alsace and Silesia magnificent large masterpieces were worked. Between

1602 and 1781 these large, heavily patterned wall hangings or carpets were produced by craftsmen for their final examinations. Possibly even used for table and bed coverings, the smallest measured over a metre square with the larger ones more than twice this size. It is not impossible that they were in fact made on wooden peg frames, but their patterning is excellent and exceedingly well placed. Of 29 known to exist before 1939 only 20 can be traced today.

RESEARCH

The time for research is not yet over and there are many questions still unanswered. It may be that a link will yet be found to explain the similarity between patterns such as those from Aran, Austria and Bavaria.

The Rev. John Brand, writing of Shetland in 1700, mentions that 'they send to Holland and Germany for fine fabrics'. Might it have been that patterns such as these from Shetland and Sweden came from a common source? Or are they accidentally alike because they are the natural outcome of what stitches will conveniently do when worked in colours? The Fairisle pattern (*9*) is dated 1850 but the border design (*10*) comes from Halstad in Sweden, where the people claim to have been taught long before that by someone who learnt in or from Holland. The links between Holland and Shetland, even long before 1700, were exceedingly strong.

There are also examples of stockings made in Albania and surrounding areas which seem to combine two

6 English sixteenth-century cap.
Victoria and Albert Museum, London

19

7 Aran half diamond pattern   8 Bavarian half diamond pattern

techniques and, although usually attributed to knitting, would seem to be more easily achieved by a form of single-needle knitting or of a type of Tunisian crochet worked with a set of long, hooked needles. Such needles are known to have existed, but have always been supposed to have been used for the formation of a knitted stitch, even if it is a crossed knitting stitch.

The complexity of the story only reflects the complexity of man. Capable of great skill, amazing artistry and endless ingenuity, he lives in an ever changing world where conflict results in changing boundaries, altered lifestyles and even in the movement of people from one land to another where the old skills may be practised afresh.

KNITTING LIVES ON

That knitting does live on after disruption and great
changes in people's way of life can be seen perfectly in
three small, lace-edged handkerchiefs (11) which were
made over 100 years ago many miles from their present
location, the American Museum in Britain, Bath.

Around 1800 the McComb Rawson family emigrated
from Scotland, settling temporarily in New York State.
But when gold was found in California in 1849 they again
took to the road, this time in a covered wagon, and along
with many others set out on the perilous journey west to
new lands and better prospects. Eventually they settled on
a ranch 18 miles west of Sacramento, California, but for
Sarah McComb Rawson it was indeed a new way of life.
Having travelled so far she was to spend the rest of her

9 Fairisle cap. *National Museum of
Antiquities of Scotland, Edinburgh*

days in a chair due to a back injury acquired while dealing with a runaway horse team. It was in this chair that she worked the fine lace which edges the handkerchiefs, lace she had first known knitted in her childhood half a century away in time and half a world away in miles. The instructions for one of the lace edgings is given in the final chapter (*page 174*).

10 Swedish pattern from Halland

11 Lace edge handkerchiefs. *The American Museum in Britain, Bath*

3 Shetland and Fairisle

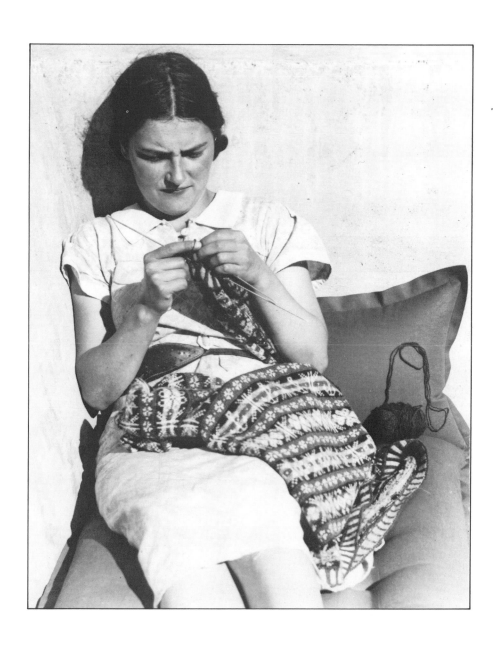

12 Shetland knitter with leather knitting belt. *National Museum of Antiquities of Scotland, Edinburgh*

There can be nowhere better suited to being the starting point for a closer look at traditional knitting than the islands of Shetland, lying between Scotland and Norway, and holding within their rocky, often storm-battered coastline a wealth of technique as well as pattern.

The Shetlanders are justly famous for their beautifully patterned knitting, but the history of their knitting should not be confused with the history of their sheep, which reaches back before the Vikings made their first landings.

SHETLAND SHEEP

Without the sheep there might be no story, for it is the fine, soft quality of their wool which makes the knitted garment unlike any others, keeping the demand for exports high.

The wool, which is not clipped from the sheep, but plucked or 'rooed' from the animal by hand, is lightly spun. Even before the advent of chemical dyes the wool was available in a wide range of natural colours, for the sheep are not only white and cream, but fawn and grey like the sea spray, dark like the peat freshly cut, or almost black. Rooeing the fleece makes for purity, for only wool is taken, without any of the hair. As early as 1612 illegal rooeing of sheep was widespread and to curtail this practice it was ordered that rooeing should be made a public occasion.

EARLY KNITTING

The earliest knitting in Shetland was not the patterns which are so well known world-wide today. By 1600 there was an immense trade in plain stockings which grew until about 1790, diminished for a period around the turn of the century, but by 1840 was reaching a new peak. By the mid-eighteenth century the number of pairs of stockings knitted for sale in Shetland was in the region of 50,000 per annum and by 1790 brought in £17,000.

Popular belief, often quoted as fact, would credit the sailors of the Spanish ship El Gran Griffon, wrecked in 1588, as the means by which the islanders, who must have been skilled knitters already, turned from plain work to creating patterns not unlike those of Spain. Technically this would not have been impossible, but there seems little to substantiate the claim and there is a strange silence on the matter from those who wrote about the islanders during the next 200 years, when they might certainly have been expected to comment on such outstanding work. However, even recent writers have not always noticed what might have been expected of them, and until there is further proof, the earliest example of patterned knitting found on Shetland is a purse found at Gunnister in 1951 which can be dated accurately to about 1690. It was here that the body of a man was dug from a peat bog and, although little remained of the man, his stockings, gloves, two caps and purse were in a comparatively good state of preservation, the purse still holding coins from Nijmegan and Overysel dated 1690 and 1681 and a Swedish coin dated 1683. He may well have been a trader from abroad, but if he was a native then his purse shows the start of Fairisle patterns in the very simple pattern of blocks and colour stripes. The coins give no proof that he came from Europe because coins from many different lands were in use at that time in Shetland, which was in no way isolated from the surrounding countries.

THE BACKGROUND
Although remote geographically these islands cannot be termed isolated as Alexander Fenton points out in his book *The Northern Isles*, for they were 'a maritime cross roads where men of many nations met and became acquainted with each other.' When he visited Bressay Sound, then, as now, the harbour for the mainland of Shetland, in 1774, Dr Rev. George Lee found over 400 vessels in the Sound, 200 of which were Dutch, the remainder being Danish, Prussian, French and Flemish. This shows something of the link with Europe and of the role of Lerwick as a market place for the island knitters whose excellent work was already greatly in demand, and was to become even more sought after towards the end of the following century.

FAIRISLE PATTERNS
'Fairisle knitting' has today become a term to cover any patterned knitting in several colours. This is totally wrong, however, and Fairisle knitting is very specialized in design and colour, even when used to include the work carried out also in Shetland.

Fair Isle, a small island to the south of the mainland of Shetland, once called the Island of Sheep, still takes pride in its knitting. Fair Isle introduced the use of dyed wool for knitting patterns before the days of chemical dyes, obtaining a deep soft rose or pale yellow and purplish brown from the lichens growing on the rocks.

The patterns the islanders have used throughout the years, often never repeating throughout a garment, can be seen in long swatches decorating the National Trust Bird Observatory. Ironically, for these they use the natural colours obtained from the sheep's fleece, which, although they pre-date dyes, are more usual today than the vegetable and lichen colourings.

□ Medium
· Dark
× Medium light
○ Light

*Fig. 8 Chart for a Fairisle purse
pattern*

TRADITION AND CHANGE

Tradition may stretch over countless years, but if it is to be alive, as knitting is today in Shetland, it cannot remain the same. Therefore the knitted designs show changes over the years. It is impossible to say that there are a certain number of basic patterns and that these never alter. There are certainly recurring shapes, but, within limits, change is endless and often very slight, each knitter bringing individuality to her work.

B

A

B

A

Fig. 9 Chart for part of a Fairisle cap pattern

□ Medium
○ Light
• Dark
× Medium light

BELOW
Fig. 11 Chart for a fisherman's cap pattern

LEFT
Fig. 10 Chart for a beret pattern

× Dark
● Medium dark
□ Medium
/ Medium light
• Light

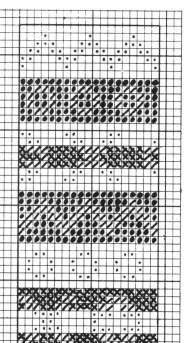

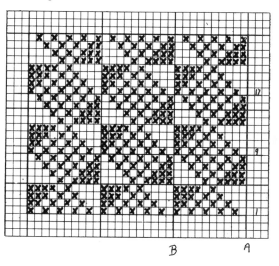

B

A

In 1850 one Fairisle pattern showed panelled patterns of hexagonal outlines with a great variety of different shapes within them, between upright, vertical and diagonal lines (*13*).

Both this and the cap (*14*) are worked in natural dyes and are blue and soft rosy red, with the pattern in yellow and white.

A beret bought in Thurso much later (*15*) still shows the use of the same type of pattern although it has been adapted for narrow bands.

A pattern which was in common use for fishermen's caps is perhaps not apparently Fairisle at all, being more like an Estonian design (*16*), but it makes a striking pattern when the first eight rows are worked in yellow and brown and the next eight rows in red and blue, alternating throughout the knitting.

The scarf (*17*), worked in brown, red, yellow and white, with pine tree motifs at either end, was made early in 1900 and again the geometric shapes predominate, but are more like an all-over pattern than the more usual clearly banded treatment.

13 Fairisle purse, dated 1850. *National Museum of Antiquities of Scotland, Edinburgh*

14 Fairisle cap, dated 1850. *National Museum of Antiquities of Scotland, Edinburgh*

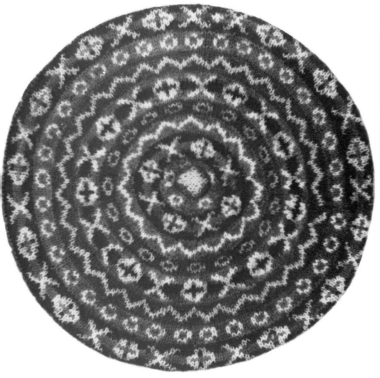

15 Fairisle beret. *National Museum of Antiquities of Scotland, Edinburgh*

16 Seaman's cap pattern

17 Shetland scarf. *National Museum of Antiquities of Scotland, Edinburgh*

Before the 1939 War a Shetland sweater might have looked like that shown here (*18*) and would have been worked in the natural sheep colours, although bright with the contrast of cream against the moorit or mid-brown and palest fawn against the darkest of all browns, which can almost pass for black. Even the ribbing would have been in two colours.

Writing in Lerwick in 1951, James Norbury, writer and designer, mentioned the Norwegian influence in Shetland patterns, which was perhaps not so early as a great many other writers have believed. Before 1939 it might have seemed natural to find Norwegian influence, because in many ways the culture of Shetland was more in tune with that of Norway than with the Scottish mainland—the ties older, the association longer. But the increase in size of the patterns used, to the larger, squarer Norwegian motif, was in fact a result of the War and can be seen in the jacket back which shows half of the pattern (*19*).

LEFT
18 A Shetlander dressed in his best.
Lerwick Museum and Library,
Shetland

19 Half back pattern of modern design

CONTINUITY

Although size and pattern may change, and change again, for there is now a marked trend back to the older style, some of the particular skills remain constant.

The use of colour, whether in dye or natural shades, never fails to give pleasure and seems to capture an ability that can never be taught or learned. There is seldom dullness, and always vivacity, even when the colours are comparatively pastel, one setting off the next, the whole a jewel of design sense.

There is also continuity, generation after generation, in placing patterns which may be appreciated, but not analysed, by others. The eye automatically appreciates evenness, not just of stitches, but of each pattern centrally fitting the shape it fills, and in all Shetland knitting pattern placing is equal, never haphazard.

Fig. 12 Chart for a large, modern pattern

TECHNIQUE

If using any yarn to its ultimate potential is the mark of success then success is to be found in Shetland. Seams which destroy the soft flexibility of the yarn are not used; where pieces must be joined, as under the arm, they are grafted, keeping the smoothness intact. Speed is essential when income is concerned and nowhere do the long needles, called 'wires' and made of steel, move more swiftly than here, where a soft leather pad is worn belted to the waist, into which the end of one needle is tucked. Nor is there constant needle changing, for only two needles hold the stitches, one for the back and one for the front, the third being used for knitting the stitches off. Even more speed can be gained by the use of circular needles, a much more recent innovation. Where colour is shaded on background or pattern, it is usual to find only two colours used at one time, although they may change frequently throughout the pattern.

Holding Yarns

Strangely, or perhaps not strangely on an island where the individual touch still matters, the method of knitting is not easy to explain. There are those who, like some European knitters, use a finger of the right hand for one colour and a finger of the left hand for the other colour, the pattern colour always being given to the hand that holds the wool less tightly so that it may sit very slightly above the background. Just across the street there is bound to be someone who puts both colours over right-hand fingers, while in North Mavine, surprisingly, they use the left hand only. Basically the work is round (not making the southern mistake of having awkward wrong-side rows to cope with) at least to the division for the armhole. Then the personal touch occurs again, for there are those who work in rows and those who continue round, cutting the work for armholes or front openings if necessary, as is the practice in Norway; there are also

Fig. 13 Holding yarn for two-colour knitting

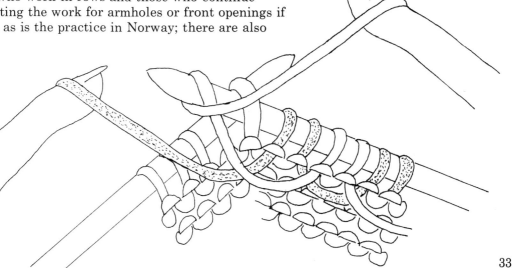

33

those who join in the already knitted sleeves and continue round to the neck, and even some who, having reached the yoke, pick up stitches for the sleeves round the armhole and work downwards to the cuff.

Stranding

Continuity is also maintained in this way of working because the colour not in use is always carried across the other stitches on the wrong side of the work (called stranding) and is never woven in by being twisted with the other colours. On traditional patterns, evolved by the knitters themselves, the width between using one colour and using it again is never great, making stranding possible. A knitting pattern that gives the knitter problems of looping yarn over ten or more stitches will almost inevitably be the inspiration of a designer.

Stranding has a very great advantage when it comes to finishing the garment, allowing the stitches freedom to even out as the wetted garment dries smooth and flat without the aid of an iron.

Finishing

The finished garment is soaked thoroughly, but is also rolled in a towel to remove excess water which would add to its weight. It is then slipped onto an adjustable frame called a board, on which it is left to dry naturally. This removes unevenness from knitting because the wool will shrink slightly as it dries, and it also draws the strands on the wrong side out evenly far more efficiently than is done by pressing, while retaining the soft feel of the yarn, also lost to some extent by hard pressing.

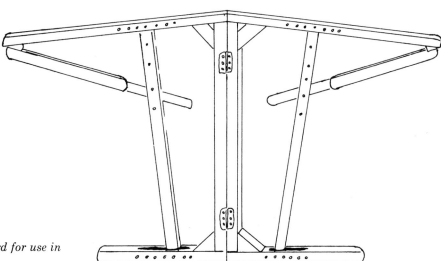

Fig. 14 A Shetland board for use in drying sweaters

Grafting

Grafting is a technique which should be known by all knitters and which once learned is neither difficult to work nor hard to remember. It can be worked in two ways, either before finishing the edges by casting off, when it is invisible and leaves no firm edges or by joining two finished edges after they have been cast off so that they appear to be seamless.

Stocking stitch

In stocking stitch, before casting off, grafting is worked by placing the two edges with wrong sides touching and with the tips of the needles both pointing to the right. Use a length of yarn left on one of the edges or join in a new length of yarn, thread the yarn into a blunt-tipped wool needle and begin at the right edge.

Insert the needle into first stitch on the front needle as if to purl and draw through the stitch, then insert needle into the first stitch on the back needle as if to knit and draw through. This is not repeated but is preparation for the first stitches only.

*Insert needle into first stitch on front needle as if to knit and draw through, slipping stitch off knitting needle tip; insert needle into next stitch on front needle as if to purl and leave it on the knitting needle; insert the needle into first stitch on back needle as if to purl and slip the stitch off the knitting needle, then insert the needle into the next stitch on the back needle as if to knit and leave it on the knitting needle, drawing the yarn through until the tension is similar to the knitting.

Repeat from * until all the stitches have been worked off, finally breaking off the yarn and darning in the end on the wrong side.

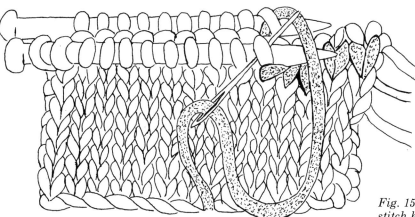

Fig. 15 Grafting, working the front stitch knitwise

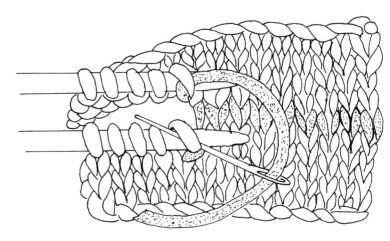

Fig. 16 Grafting, working the front stitch purlwise

Ribbing

In ribbing the simplest method is to work knit and purl stitches separately. Slip all knit stitches for the front section onto one needle and back stitches onto another. Work these as for stocking stitch grafting. Now slip all the remaining stitches onto two needles, turn the work inside out so that the purl stitches now appear as knit stitches and work them in the same way as the first side.

Garter Stitch

To graft garter stitch the rows must be facing as shown in fig. 17 with ridged rows both facing forward on each needle.

They can then both be worked in the same way as the front stitches were worked for stocking stitch.

To prepare the first stitches draw the thread through the front stitch as if to purl and repeat this through the first stitch on the back needle.

*Insert the needle through the first stitch on the front needle as if to knit and slip it off the knitting needle, then draw it through the next stitch on the front needle as if to purl; insert it into the first stitch on the back needle as if to knit and slip the stitch off the knitting needle, then draw it through the next stitch on the back needle as if to purl, leaving the stitch on the knitting needle.

Repeat from * until all the stitches have been worked.

Vertical Grafting

Side edges of knitted sections can also be joined seamlessly although there are no loops to work through.

Thread a wool needle and lift alternately one strand from one stitch in on one edge and one strand from one stitch in on the other edge until the seam is closed, taking care not to draw the yarn tight and distort the tension of the stitches on either side. The yarn must be tight enough so that the stitches cannot be drawn apart but they should sit neatly together, showing no seam. On fine

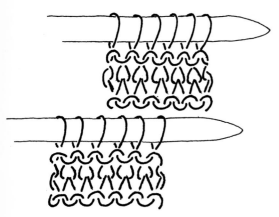

Fig. 17 Ready for grafting garter stitch

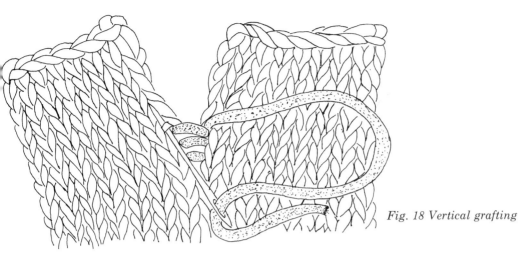

Fig. 18 Vertical grafting

knitting the needle can be passed under two threads at one time on either side.

Horizontal Grafting

Edges that have both been cast off as at shoulder seams can be joined in a similar way by lifting one complete stitch from one side then passing the needle under both strands of a complete stitch on the other side and drawing both together, before completing the next two stitches in the same way.

In Shetland, however, the stitches are always left on the needles until ready for grafting so that the shoulders are seamless.

PATTERN BOOKS

Patterns in Shetland were handed on from mother to daughter, aunt to niece or friend to friend and were remembered visually with no need of written instructions. However, many knitters, as their experience grew, kept note of their own patterns and variations in a book of squared paper, often showing the pattern in one colour only and leaving the imagination free to interpret it in a different way the next time it was used.

The following patterns might be used in just the same way to start a collection of patterns that can be added to, altered, varied and worked together in different ways.

Bands of Pattern

Patterns, even when they are worked all over a garment, may consist of varied widths of pattern combined to create a design which the knitter has used many times, or as an experiment to try a new combination.

These three borders (*20*) may be found on one garment between wider bands, or only one may be selected and used alternately with a wider band. For easy

37

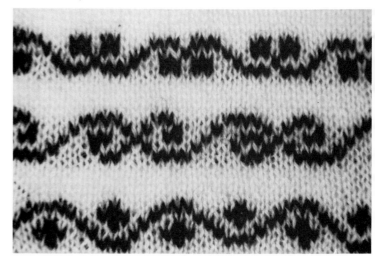

20 The brothers, the cleeks and
the sisters

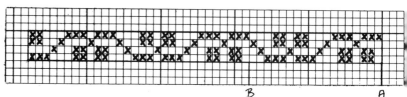

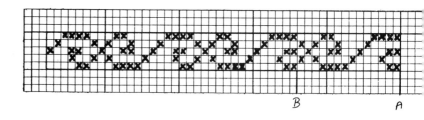

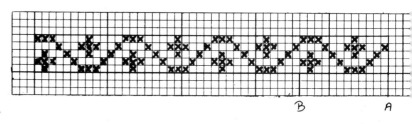

*Fig. 19 Charts for the brothers,
the cleeks and the sisters*

identification they are known from top downwards as
1 The brothers
2 The cleeks
3 The sisters.

Bands of Natural Colours
This is part of a design used by Miss Janet Petrie in 1935
for a fine garment with many variations alternating
narrow and wide patterns (*21*).

Fig. 20 Chart for Janet Petrie's design

21 Pattern by Miss Janet Petrie

The colours used were natural and moorit, grey, cream and dark brown, each narrow pattern using moorit on natural, the wide bands having at least three colour changes.

More Modern Shapes

Curves, which are a little less usual, are combined in different ways to make a beautifully balanced pattern.

Worked in bright colours, the original used one colour on the background colour for the narrow bands and changed the centre row of the wide band from the other rows using red, white, green and natural.

Crossed Band

A pattern panel need not be repeated all over a sweater and many garments are only edged with pattern on body and sleeves.

Again the panel can be coloured to suit the knitter's purpose, shading inwards or outwards from the centre.

Traditional Bands

Another filling for the traditional geometric shapes is shown here (*24*) with very narrow bands separating it from slightly wider bands before the entire pattern is repeated.

22 Curved pattern lines

Fig. 21 *Chart for curved line patterns*

23 Crossed band

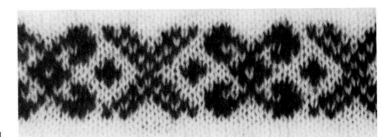

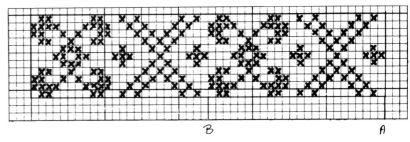

Fig. 22 *Chart for crossed band*

B   A

40

Fig. 23 Chart for traditional bands

B   A

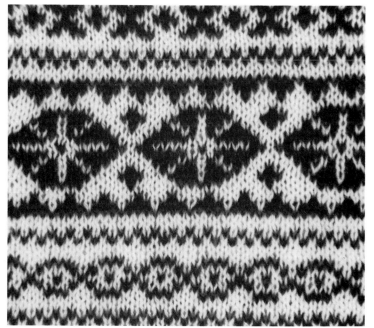

24 Traditional bands

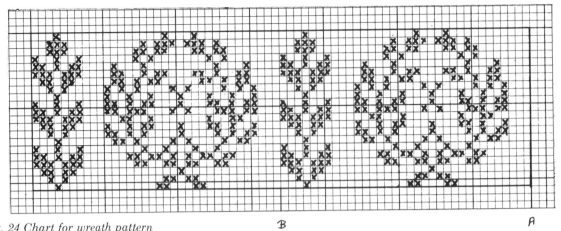

Fig. 24 Chart for wreath pattern

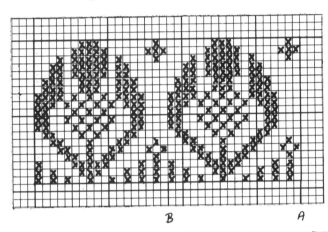

Fig. 25 Chart for thistles

Fig. 26 Chart for all-over pattern

42

25 All-over pattern

Variations
Some knitters may be content to experiment with colours, using patterns that they have used for many years, while others are always ready to try a new shape or investigate the possibilities of repeating well known shapes, such as flower petals, clover leaves, thistles or pine trees.

All-over Patterns
Bands are not the only method of creating design and many designs are based on the eight-pointed star, so much used in Norwegian knitting.

These designs always have an added bonus because the repeat creates shapes within shapes, often not noticed in a single repeat of the design.

Norwegian Influence
Ideas for designs are all around the knitter, and a good eye for shape and colour does not always use the expected source of design.

In this delightful all-over pattern (26) there was certainly Norwegian influence although not directly from a Norwegian knitting pattern. It was, in fact, taken from a linoleum design and was originally knitted in bright light green, pink and yellow on a dark brown background. It may not sound attractive, but it made a most unusual and pleasing design and has been used many times since.

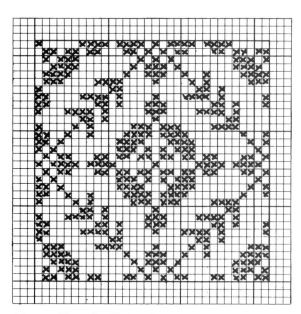

Fig. 27 Chart for Norwegian-type pattern

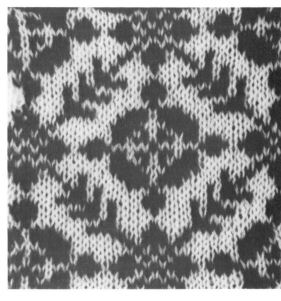

26 Norwegian influence, if indirectly

Snowflake Square

The square designs from Norway have been given Shetland's own look by being worked in beautifully shaded colours, often subtle and unexpected.

☐ White   ╱ Green
• Black   × Blue
╲ Gold   ■ Scarlet

Fig. 28 Chart for snowflake design

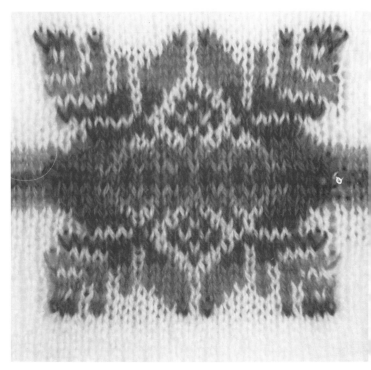

27 Snowflake square

44

Selbu Star

Although the eight-pointed star, sometimes called a flower, is by far the most usual pattern to be used from Norway, the Selbu star is becoming a close rival. In Norway it is worked in one colour on a contrasting background, dark on light or light on dark, but in Shetland it is shaded in to a dark centre or from a light centre to dark outer edges.

☐ White
• Brown
＼ Gold
／ Light brown
× Green
■ Scarlet

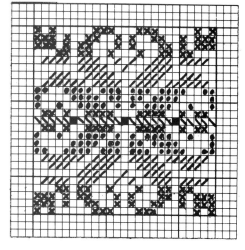

Fig. 29 Chart for Selbu star

28 Selbu star

BELOW
Fig. 30 Chart for checked stocking pattern

LEFT
29 Stocking checked pattern

Checked Pattern

Shetland knitters have for a very long time made stockings, many of which are worked in more than one colour. The checked patterns used are very easy to knit and can

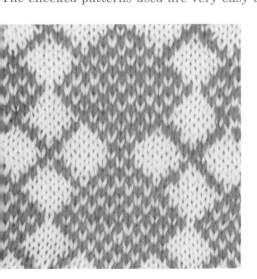

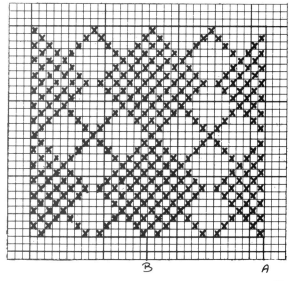

B   A

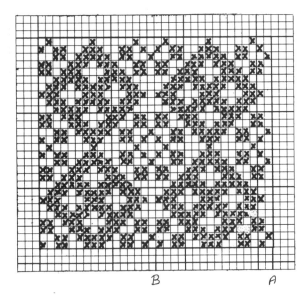

Fig. 31 Chart for diamond and flower pattern

30 Diamond and flower stocking pattern

be used for other garments also. These are worked in the same way as other types of coloured knitting, by stranding the yarn across the back of the work.

Diamond and Flower

Worked in fine yarn in natural and dark brown, this pattern makes a fine pair of stockings.

Checked Diamond and Flower

This is a variation composed of parts of both of the two previous patterns.

Fig. 32 Chart for checked diamond and flower

31 Checked diamond and flower pattern

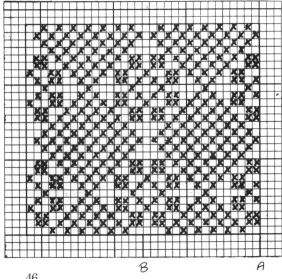

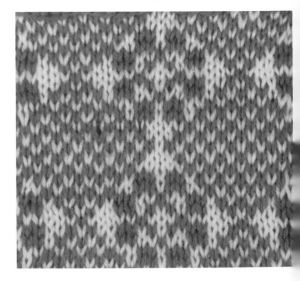

LACE KNITTING

Lace knitting with very fine yarns, as worked on the most northerly island of Unst, is dealt with in Chapter 9, but Shetland is also famous for many other lace patterns which are not used in Unst knitting.

The shawls of Shetland are the best-known form of lace knitting and were worked not only in natural self-colours but often with the wide borders inside the edging lace pattern in shaded bands of pastel colours, or shades of the natural colours of greys, browns and creams, which are probably more popular today.

Like all Shetland work the wool is used to its best advantage and the softness of the finished item never spoilt by hard seam lines. The shawls were knitted from the edge inwards, with as many edges as possible picked up from other edges, thus reducing the number of seams required. They were finished by drying on frames to avoid pressing.

Both a scarf and a shawl can be made in the traditional way from the instructions on pages 174, 175.

LACE PATTERNS

The traditional patterns of Shetland are as simple as any

32 Finishing shawls in Lerwick.
Lerwick Museum

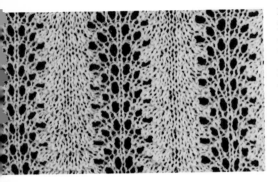

33 Old shale pattern

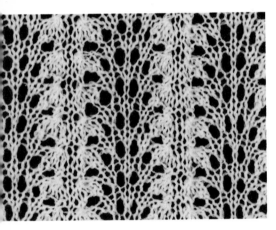

34 Feather and fan pattern

35 Crest of the wave pattern

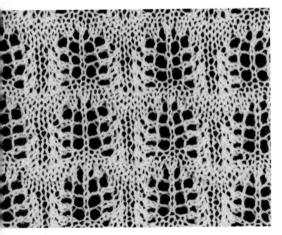

that can be found throughout the world and none are more beautiful. Often based on garter stitch, they never include awkward techniques or unusual methods of working. Basically they are constructed with holes made by putting the yarn over the needle which is compensated for at the same point or elsewhere in the row by taking two stitches together. When three stitches are taken together they may be worked by slipping the first, taking the other two together and lifting the first stitch over the ones taken together, but this is likely to be the most difficult movement used and is more commonly worked by simply knitting three stitches together.

Old Shale Pattern
A design which certainly recalls the pattern of the waves on the beach on a calm day, this is also a pattern from which many variations are derived and which lends itself to being worked in shaded colours as well as in only one colour. The islanders refer to it as the shell pattern.

Worked over a number of sts divisible by 18, plus 1.
1st row *K1, [K2 tog] 3 times, [yon, K1] 5 times, yon, [K2 tog] 3 times, rep from * to last st, K1.
2nd row K.
3rd row K.
4th row P.
Rep 1st–4th rows as required.

Feather and Fan Pattern
This is similar to the previous pattern, but the stitches decreased are clustered more closely together or feathered.

Cast on a number of sts divisible by 14, plus 1.
1st row *K1, K4 tog, [yon, K1] 5 times, yon, sl 2, K2 tog, p2sso, rep from * to last st, K1.
2nd row *K4, P7, K3, rep from * to last st, K1.
3rd row K.
4th row P.
Rep 1st–4th rows as required.

Crest of the Wave Pattern
Again this is a pattern which lends itself to colour change, and, like so many of the patterns, it is easy to remember.

Cast on a number of sts divisible by 12, plus 1.
1st and 2nd rows K.
3rd row P.
4th row K.
5th row *K1, [K2 tog] twice, [yon, K1] 3 times, yon, [K2 tog tbl] twice, rep from * to last st, K1.

6th row P.
7th–12th rows Rep 5th and 6th rows 3 times.
Rep 1st–12th rows as required.

Bead Stitch
A basic stitch, this too has many forms and is often used
without so many stitches between the clustered stitches.
In this form it seems to live up to its name with openwork
beads between more solid areas.

Cast on a number of sts divisible by 9.
1st row *K2, K2 tog, yon, K1, yon, K2 tog, K2, rep from *
to end.
2nd row *K1, K2 tog, yon, K3, yon, K2 tog, K1, rep from *
to end.
3rd row *K2, yon, K2 tog, K1, K2 tog, yon, K2, rep from *
to end.
4th row *K3, yon, K3 tog, yon, K3, rep from * to end.
Rep 1st–4th rows as required.

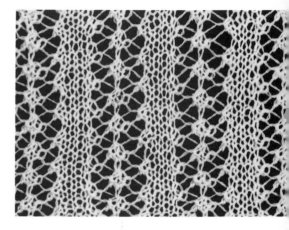

36 Bead stitch

Cat's Paw Pattern
This pattern is so called because it is just like the marks
left by a cat walking over a newly washed floor or freshly
raked garden border.

Cast on a number of sts divisible by 11.
1st row *K3, K2 tog, yon, K1, yon, K2 tog tbl, K3, rep
from * to end.
2nd row P.
3rd row *K2, K2 tog, yon, K3, yon, K2 tog tbl, K2, rep
from * to end.
4th row P.
5th row *K4, yon, sl 1, K2 tog, psso, yon, K4, rep from * to
end.
6th row P.
Rep 1st–6th rows as required.

37 Cat's paw pattern

Mrs Hunter's Pattern
Delightfully different in its precise openwork pattern, this
can be a most useful stitch, alone, or to set off more
complex patterns.

Cast on a number of sts divisible by 4, plus 2.
1st row K.
2nd row P.
3rd row K1, *sl 1, K3, pass sl st over the K3, rep from * to
last st, K1.
4th row P1, *P3, yon, rep from * to last st, P1.
Rep 1st–4th rows as required.

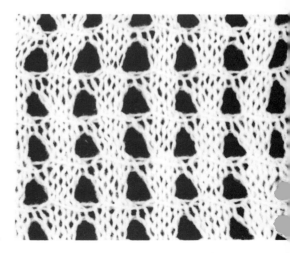

38 Mrs Hunter's pattern

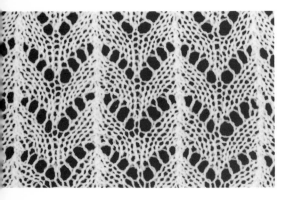

39 Horseshoe lace

Horseshoe Pattern

Variations of this pattern can be found in many countries but it is always worked in a simple form in Shetland.

Cast on a number of sts divisible by 10, plus 1.

1st row P.

2nd row K1, *yon, K3, sl 1, K2 tog, psso, K3, yon, K1, rep from * to end.

3rd row P.

4th row P1, *K1, yon, K2, sl 1, K2 tog, psso, K2, yon, K1, P1, rep from * to end.

5th row K1, *P9, K1, rep from * to end.

6th row P1, *K2, yon, K1, sl 1, K2 tog, psso, K1, yon, K2, P1, rep from * to end.

7th row K1, *P9, K1, rep from * to end.

8th row P1, *K3, yon, sl 1, K2 tog, psso, yon, K3, P1, rep from * to end.

Rep 1st–8th rows as required.

Razor Shell Pattern

This is a convenient pattern because it can be altered in width so very easily from the narrowest of ribs to a wide chevron.

Cast on a number of sts divisible by 6, plus 1.

1st row P.

2nd row K1, *yon, K1, sl 1, K2 tog, psso, K1, yon, K1, rep from * to end.

Rep 1st and 2nd rows as required.

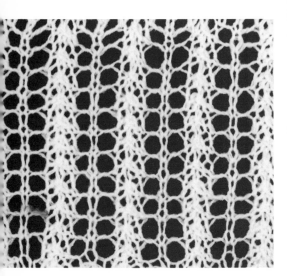

40 Razor shell pattern

4 Britain

The earliest knitting recorded in Britain is unfortunately not likely to have been made by British knitters, but brought or sent to Britain from Spain. However, in 1488 an Act of Parliament was passed setting the price of both felted and woollen caps, so these must have been made in comparative quantities for some time previously.

It must be remembered that knitting was often used to augment otherwise slender incomes and, as a means to an end, was worked quickly and in every odd moment. Stockings, caps and gloves were amongst the first items produced and these were undoubtedly plain, unpatterned work. Patterning came much later, when knitting became a domestic hobby rather than a way of earning a living.

It is hardly surprising that the stocking frame eventually took precedence over hand knitting as a source of income. Nevertheless, knitting lived on in rural areas, and gradually many of the patterns that are still in use were developed. It is interesting to note that in a petition to the Protector, Oliver Cromwell, in 1651, it is pointed out that the imports from foreign knitters harmed the hand knitter more than the work of the frame knitters.

DALE KNITTING

Few examples are left of the large trade in hand-knitted goods once carried on by the men, women and children in the Dales of Yorkshire, where even in 1814 George Walker was able to find material for an illustration in his book *Costumes of Yorkshire*. As in most countries where knitting has augmented a meagre income, knitting was carried in the hand, and worked while walking from one place to another, losing no opportunity to gain a few rounds.

BORDER KNITTING

Gloves made with fine checked patterns, not unlike those occasionally found in the north-west of England, were also knitted in the Scottish border area of Sanquhar, near Dumfries, which is famous for its designs.

The patterns which are recognized most easily today as being Sanquhar patterns are small blocks and diamonds of two contrasting colours, but were preceded by smaller patterns almost echoing the patterns to be found in woven tweeds. Worked on very fine needles, the smooth yarn showed the pattern to perfection and was often edged at the wrist with a rib using the two colours together, one for the purl stitches, the other for the plain stitches. Dark grey or brown was often used for one colour with pale blue, lemon or creamy white as the other, although early in the nineteenth century a rosy red and a soft green reminiscent of ancient tartans were also used.

42 Sanquhar check

52

43(a) Driving gloves. *Lerwick Museum*

BELOW
43(b) Construction of the driving gloves. *Lerwick Museum*

Knitted throughout the nineteenth century and revived more recently by the publication of knitting instructions by the Scottish Women's Rural Industries in Edinburgh, these patterns must have been knitted in even larger quantities before the end of the eighteenth century. In the First Statistical Account for this area written in 1793 it is clearly recorded that the knitting of Sanquhar was declining by 1790.

Sanquhar Check
This check is one of the later designs but was in use by about 1830 and may have been considerably earlier.

The chart shows one repeat plus two extra stitches required to make it central.

Driving Gloves
A similar check is used for these driving gloves (*43, 44*) which come from Shetland and which are ingenious in their construction, giving maximum warmth for the hands

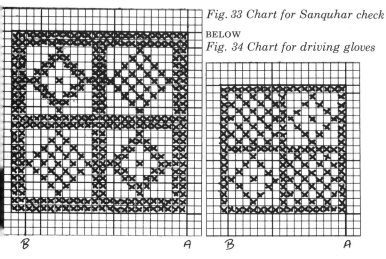

Fig. 33 Chart for Sanquhar check

BELOW
Fig. 34 Chart for driving gloves

53

holding the reins. The fingerless section is worked in one with the rest of the glove and is folded back across the fingers in wear, giving the bonus of a doubled wrist area.

Fig. 34 shows the framed repeat with the one extra stitch required to make the pattern central.

ARGYLL PATTERNED HOSE

Knitting has always been used for head, hand and leg coverings because of the ease with which it can be shaped, and endless patterns can be found to substantiate this fact. In Scotland, however, the need for a particular type of stocking also meant a technique for coloured work different from knitting in rounds to produce a seamless, comfortable garment.

The type of stocking worn with the kilt, particularly by military regiments, is worked either in large checks, showing light, dark and a half-toned area between, usually worked with a marled yarn, or patterns checked like tartan. Because the yarn would have to be carried over many stitches from one colour point to the next it is not possible to work in the usual way.

Working on two needles instead of four, a separate length of yarn must be used for each colour area.

For the first row of the chart in fig. 35 the instructions would read as follows:

K1B using 1st ball of B, 7A using 1st ball of A, 1C using 1st ball of C, 7A using 2nd ball of A, 1B using 2nd ball of B, 1B again using 3rd ball of B (these 2 stitches cannot be

44 Tartan hose, Argyll pattern

Fig. 35 Chart for tartan Argyll pattern

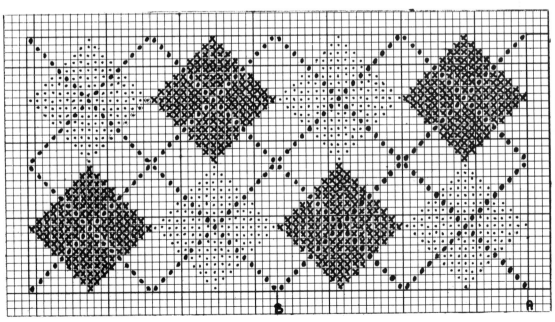

A □
B ●
C ·
D ×

worked from the same ball because on subsequent rows they separate and with single strands for each line there is no need to carry the yarn as would be the case if 1 ball were used), 7A using 3rd ball of A, 1D using 1st ball of D, 7A using 4th ball of A, 1B using 4th ball of B, 1B using 5th ball of B, 7A using 5th ball of A, 1C using 2nd ball of C, 7A using 6th ball of A, 1B using 6th ball of B, 1B using 7th ball of B, 7A using 7th ball of A, 1D using 2nd ball of D, 7A using 8th ball of A, 1B using 8th ball of B.

Knitting with Small Balls

This is not as fearsome a task as it sounds, nor need knitting be difficult with balls continually tangling.

Wind small quantities of each yarn onto card bobbins similar in shape to the letter H (*fig. 36*). Balls which are fixed in any way, by spearing with a needle or confining to tins or small boxes, will still tangle as they are used because they are not free to jump clear of each other. Yarn wound onto light cards will be able to move as the cards are jerked to obtain more yarn, and will disentangle themselves.

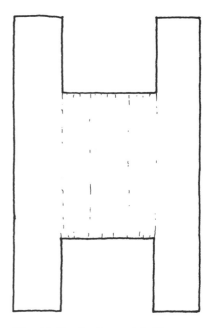

Fig. 36 Shape of a card bobbin

Changing Colour

When small lengths of yarn or small balls are used to work a colour area that is too large to have strands drawn across the wrong side, the colours must be twisted together at colour change points, to avoid unnecessary gaps in the fabric on the right side. The yarn which has been used is laid to the left and the yarn that is going to be used is brought up over it to work the first stitch of that colour. The same method is used in working wrong-side rows, with the yarns twisted on the wrong side of the fabric resulting in neatly joined areas that lie without wrinkles. It is also more economical for yarn quantities for none is used travelling from one point to another. This method is not only used for tartan knitting, but can be employed wherever colours need to be carried over more than five or seven stitches.

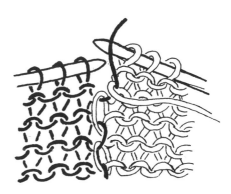

Fig. 37 Twisting one yarn round the other

FISHERMEN'S KNITTING

All round the coast of Britain a tradition of knitting grew up which, although less used today, is still practised by many, while others benefit from the wealth of pattern it has left behind.

Fishermen's guernseys or 'ganseys' as they are known in English ports, began life in the Channel Islands, hence their name. In Guernsey fishermen's sweaters were made from Elizabethan times and became quite an extensive trade, particularly to Newfoundland. Although the name was adopted in England, the Channel Island garment is not patterned as the English version so often is, except for

45 Waiting for action. *Shipley Art Gallery, Newcastle*

the small changes in texture at either side of the chest and above the garter stitch welt (*see fig. 168*).

At one time it was true to say that a fisherman could be identified, at least as far as the locality he came from, by the pattern of his guernsey. Later this became more difficult to do, as travel became easier and as more garments were seen by knitters.

In Scotland the herring lasses, who travelled to the English ports to clean the herring and to look after the men, admitted that they were always ready to attempt any pattern that they saw which took their fancy and seemed to be an improvement on the patterns they already used.

Vertical patterns have always been popular for they are particularly easy to plan to gain the correct size. Patterned with purled stitches on plain or with complex looking cables, like the fishermens' own ropes, the variety of pattern is seemingly endless, texture and design always playing an important part.

BRITISH PATTERNS

Garter Stitch and Cable Pattern

A simple design, this straightforward cable pattern is enhanced by the clear vertical lines of the garter stitch panels between the purl lines linking the panels together.

Cast on a number of sts divisible by 20. An extra panel of 6 sts will be needed if the pattern is to be worked on 2 needles.

1st round *P1, K2, P1, K6, P1, K2, P1, K6, rep from * to end.
2nd round P4, K6, P4, K6, rep from * to end.
3rd round Work as for 1st round.
4th round Work as for 2nd round.
5th round *P1, K2, P1, sl next 3 sts to CN, hold at back, K3, K3 from CN, P1, K2, P1, K6, rep from * to end.
6th round Work as for 2nd round.
7th and 8th rounds Work as for 1st and 2nd rounds.
Rep these 8 rounds as required.

46 Garter stitch and cable pattern

Church Windows

Many patterns have their own names, either because the knitters set out to create patterns derived from everyday life or because the pattern the stitches took reminded them of paths and rocks, of sand and waves or, as in this case, of the small window panes in the church. This pattern comes from Fraserburgh near Aberdeen, in Scotland.

Cast on a number of sts divisible by 21.
1st round *K1, [P1, K5] twice, P1, K1, P1, K4, P1, rep from * to end.
2nd round Work as for 1st round.
3rd round *K2, [P1, K3, P1, K1] twice, K1, P1, sl next st to CN, hold at back, K1, K1 from CN, sl next st to CN, hold at front, K1, K1 from CN, P1, rep from * to end.
4th round *K2, [P1, K3, P1, K1] twice, K1, P1, K4, P1, rep from * to end.
5th round *K3, [P1, K1, P1, K3] twice, P1, K4, P1, rep from * to end.
6th round Work as for 5th round.
7th round *K4, P1, K5, [P1, K4] twice, P1, rep from * to end.
8th round Work as for 7th round.
9th round *K3, [P1, K1, P1, K3] twice, P1, sl next st to CN, hold at back, K1, K st from CN, sl next st to CN, hold at front, K1, K st from CN, P1, rep from * to end.
10th round Work as for 5th round.
11th and 12th rounds Work as for 4th round.
Rep these 12 rounds as required.

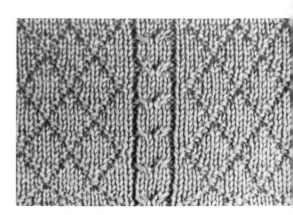

47 Church windows pattern

Marriage Lines

Twin lines, said to reflect the ups and downs of married life are often worked into pattern panels.

Because fishermen's guernseys are traditionally knitted round, and to allow for either round knitting or flat knitting on two needles, the pattern is best shown on a chart catering for either type of knitting. The purl stitches which provide the pattern on the right side of stocking stitch are shown as crosses on the chart, which shows two complete pattern repeats.

One complete repeat uses 18 stitches.

Fig. 38 Chart for marriage lines pattern

RIGHT
48 Marriage lines

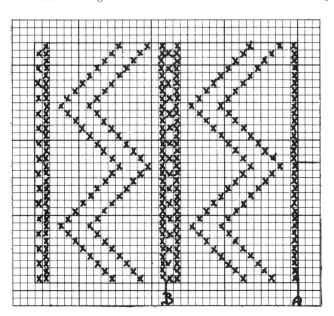

Lightning and Steps

Single diagonal lines are said to represent lightning with the dividing panel reminiscent of the steps up the cliff sides of many a village from harbour or shore to the safety of home.

The pattern repeat requires 20 stitches.

Sheringham Pattern

Like the brocade knitted in silk during the time of Charles I, this pattern from Norfolk uses the familiar moss with single moss diamonds, with a variation in the solid block in place of the complete moss diamond.

The pattern repeats over 24 stitches.

Yoked Patterns

Many patterns were not all over the guernsey but were worked as only a yoke. The yoke varied in depth and was often framed in horizontal lines of several purl rows followed by several plain rows, alternated over a few

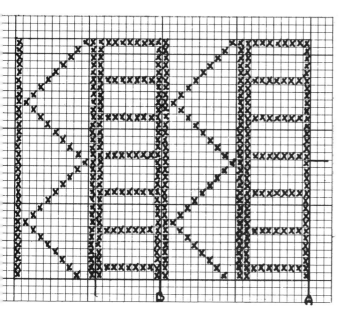

49 Lightning and steps

Fig. 39 Chart for lightning and steps pattern

ridges. This particular example (*51*) shows clearly the shoulders which were always cast off together and on the right side, forming a neat ridge and avoiding a seam.

50 Sheringham pattern

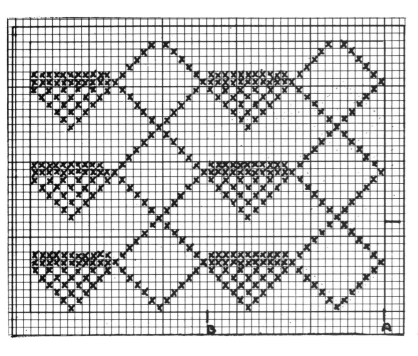

Fig. 40 Chart for Sheringham pattern

THE SEAMLESS TECHNIQUE

Worked round to avoid seams, guernseys, although
varying in pattern, had many factors in common,
wherever they came from. Shoulders were usually cast off
to form a neat line on the right side and extra gussets
were usually worked under the sleeves at the armhole, the
sleeves themselves being picked up around the armhole
and knitted downwards to the wrist.

Knitters today recall that guernseys were always cast
on using double yarn for extra strength. Unfortunately
the full meaning of this seems to have been lost and many
patterns that have been revived have been spoilt by an
ugly edge with large loops made from casting on using
two strands of yarn. In fact there are several ways of
casting on which do neaten, strengthen and decorate the
lower edge.

Channel Islands Casting On

The method of casting on used in the Channel Islands
uses two strands for the yarn looped round the thumb, but
knits the loop of the stitch with a single strand.

Cut two strands of yarn three times as long as the edge
to be cast on. Using one needle only wrap the doubled
yarn round the thumb anticlockwise. Insert the needle,
held in the right hand under all four strands on the thumb
and use the single end of yarn to the ball to knit the first
stitch. Put the yarn (single) over the needle as for an
increase, making the second stitch. For the third stitch

OPPOSITE
51 Fisherman with yoked sweater.
*The Scottish Fisheries Museum,
Anstruther*

61

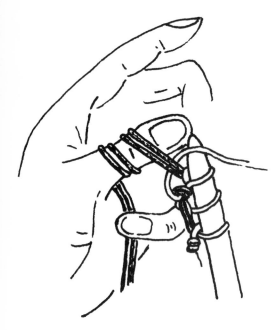

again pick up the four strands of yarn from the thumb and using the single yarn make a loop on the needle. Continue in this way until the required number are cast on, working one stitch over the needle and one through the thumb loops alternately. This automatically means ending with an odd number of stitches, but if necessary one can be decreased or increased if an even number is required.

Knotted Edge Cast On
The knotted-edge cast on is worked using only one strand of yarn but knots the stitches in such a way that it makes the edge firm and hard wearing.

Using the thumb method cast on two stitches. Using the left needle tip, lift the first stitch over the second and off the needle, leaving one stitch on right needle.

*Cast on two more stitches using the thumb method, lift first over second and off the needle, leaving two stitches on right needle. Rep from * until the required number of stitches has been cast on.

This knotted edge can also be seen in use on the guernsey for which there are instructions on page 167.

Fig. 41 Wrapping the yarn twice round the thumb for Channel Islands cast on

RIGHT
52 Lifting one stitch over the next in knotted edge cast on

53 Knotted edge casting on

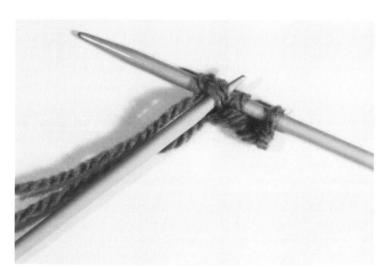

62

5 Aran

Remote from the bustle of city life, inaccessible during rough weather, where the setting sun seems to dip into the rollers sweeping in from the Atlantic, lie the Aran islands, off the mouth of Galway Bay in the extreme west of Ireland.

On the main islands of Inishmore, the big island, Inishmaan, the middle island, and Inisheer, the west island, are knitters today who still knit the stitch patterns handed down from mother and grandmother, kept alive by generation following generation.

BAININ

Fashion's dictate brings Aran yarn in many colours but for the islander it is the natural creamy colour which gives the yarn its name of Bainin, pronounced *bawneen* and meaning 'natural'. In this natural wool the light and shade formed by the stitch patterns is seen to advantage with its wealth of textures and endless possibilities for variation.

These textures bring another dimension into knitting, with the depth of shadow created by honeycomb and lattice, by cable and diamond. Here is a wealth of pattern at odds to a life of toil for a meagre return from the soil, often barely covering the rocks and the sea, seldom calm and tranquil.

PATTERNS FROM LIFE

Today the patterns that have been handed down from expert to novice seem to reflect the lives of the islanders, with stitches named after the small stone-walled fields of the west, the fishermen's ropes, the lobsters round the rocky shores and the symbols of their religion, such as Trinity stitch (the Three in One and One in Three) or the Tree of Life stitch, said to ensure long life to the wearer and strong sons to help with the fishing.

These heavily embossed patterns, possibly also their symbolism, have evolved throughout the years and are now more complex than they once were. In this design (55) the vertical lines of ribbing give way to the smoothness of stocking stitch which in turn serves as the perfect background for the most traditional of all patterns, moss stitch, which is used in so many ways to create surface interest, as fillings for other shapes or to contrast against smooth areas.

DESIGN

The islander knitting for husband and sons was able to adapt and use pattern without feeling the need to write down the movements of stitches. Creating one individual size, fingers and eye worked together to achieve contrast,

55 An example of an early Aran pattern

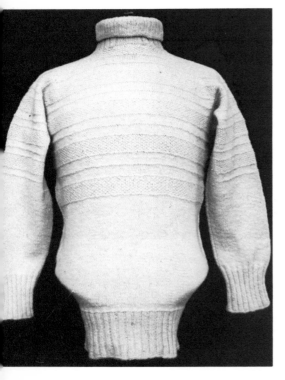

drawing on skill and memory for inspiration, always able to try a new arrangement when the idea occurred. These patterns were often complex (56). The front of the sweater differs considerably from the back and consists of a central panel extended into a diamond pattern instead of a triangle, flanked on either side by a deeply embossed rib and with zig zag side panels echoing the slope of the lattice used on the front. The bobble used to highlight the front triangles is repeated at either side of each diamond on the back, giving a strongly related design. As in all earlier sweaters the sleeves are set in and are used to link the back and front patterns, carrying a central panel of the back embossed cable. The patterned welt used on sleeves and back as well as on the front, serves to unite the other textures into a complete design.

Both centre back diamond and embossed cable have been used in the design given on page 154.

The tradition of Aran knitting is unique and unlike many other island methods each section is worked separately, and the garment seamed on completion of knitting.

Basically the designs were pieced together round a central panel flanked by vertical lines, often cables, before a side panel completed the area. Where back and front were different they were always related, in direction or in shape, in texturing or type of pattern.

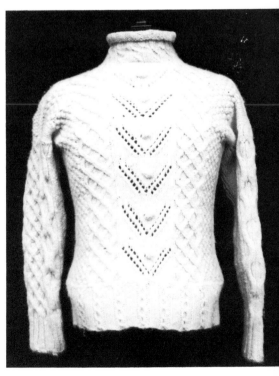

56 Lace-fronted Aran sweater, showing bobble and triangle pattern. *The National Museum, Dublin*

This relation between one pattern and another can be seen in the photographs (57, 58) showing the back and front of the same sweater.

Both central panels use a diamond pattern but with quite different fillings. Either side of the centre panel shows a similar sized vertical pattern but on one it is a cable while on the other a narrow column of honeycomb pattern. On the shoulder edge the outer cable is used on all sections, front and back, and is repeated on the sleeves and collar; cuffs and welt unite the design with the Tree of Life pattern, echoing the slanting lines of diamond and zig zag lines.

In some designs this structure has been lost, and it is interesting to note that where central panels and filled diamonds have given way to related vertical cables, composed of single-twist stitches, often separated by lines of single-twisted stitches, something much nearer the Bavarian and Austrian style of patterning is found. Whether this is due to influence or whether each evolved completely separately is hard to clarify.

Commercialization, bringing with it the need to rationalize patterns and to knit for a market dealing in many different sizes, inevitably brings loss of freedom of design. The knitter today, sitting at her cottage front

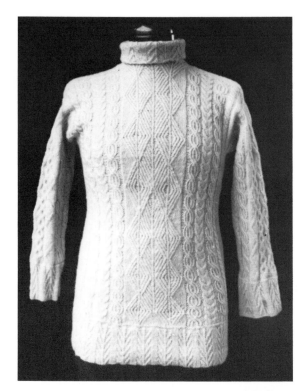
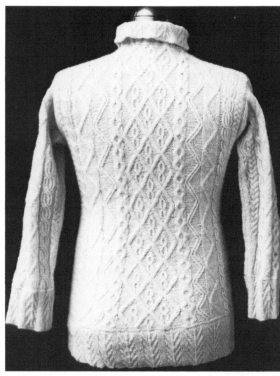

57 and **58** Front and back of Aran sweater. *The National Museum, Dublin*

59 Sweater showing Honeycomb and Trinity stitch panels. *The National Museum, Dublin*

door, knits a raglan-sleeved sweater, which carries simplified panels allowing for the addition or reduction of side panel or central panel stitches to make a design suitable for a large size range. The use of a small honeycomb pattern at the side of the sweater (59) and a central panel of Trinity stitch, retains texture and main side panels but allows for easy size alterations in these smaller stitch patterns.

Bobbles

Bobbles can be used in several ways but are at their best when they emphasize the design, underlining, as it were, an important point. They can lose their usefulness if they get out of hand both from the design point of view and from the knitter's outlook in tackling their construction.

60 Sweater showing good use of bobbles. *The National Museum, Dublin*
BELOW
61 What happens with too many bobbles. *The National Museum, Dublin*

ARAN PATTERNS

The following patterns are from designs once knitted in Aran but possibly less seen today because of the need, in many cases, to provide instructions either for several sizes easily read from the same pattern or because of the length of the repeat and the amount of space taken up by the necessary instructions.

Abbreviations

Unique patterns call for their own abbreviations and standard abbreviations are seldom sufficient for Aran designs. This does not mean that they are more difficult to knit, but simply that many cables or travelling stitches need to be given a personal abbreviation.

Where abbreviations apply only to one stitch pattern they have been placed before that actual pattern. There are some exceptions where a basic twist to right or left is

67

used or a simple cable is involved, and these can be found in the main list of abbreviations in Chapter 1.

Where crossed stitches are concerned, moving only one position but worked through the back of the stitch for additional effect, the knitter will find that most can be worked without a cable needle, but because some crosses are awkward all have been treated as cables using the aid of an extra needle.

These are abbreviated as follows:
Cr2FK   sl next st to CN, hold at front, P1, Kb1 from CN
Cr2BP   sl next st to CN, hold at back, Kb1, P1 from CN.
Cr2FKb   sl next st to CN, hold at front, Kb1, Kb1 from CN.
Cr2BKb   sl next st to CN, hold at back, Kb1, Kb1 from CN.

Patterned welt stitches make use of simple travelling stitch patterns or small cables.

62 Zig zag welt pattern

Zig Zag Welt
Worked over a number of sts divisible by 7.
1st row *K4, Kb1, P2, rep from * to end.
2nd row *K2, Pb1, P4, rep from * to end.
3rd row *K4, Cr2FK, P1, rep from * to end.
4th row *K1, Pb1, K1, P4, rep from * to end.
5th row *K4, P1, Cr2FK, rep from * to end.
6th row *Pb1, K2, P4, rep from * to end.
7th row *K4, P1, Cr2BP, rep from * to end.
8th row *K1, Pb1, K1, P4, rep from * to end.
9th row *K4, Cr2BP, P1, rep from * to end.
Rep 2nd–9th rows as required.

63 Slanting welt pattern

Slanting Welt
This is like the first part of zig zag welt with the slanted stitch travelling in one direction only, not returning in the reverse direction as in zig zag welt.

Worked over a number of sts divisible by 6.
1st row *K3, Kb1, P2, rep from * to end.
2nd row *K2, Pb1, P3, rep from * to end.
3rd row *K3, Cr2FK, P1, rep from * to end.
4th row *K1, P1, K1, P3, rep from * to end.
5th row *K3, P1, Cr2FK, rep from * to end.
6th row *Pb1, K2, P3, rep from * to end.
Rep 1st–6th rows as required.

Tree of Life Welt (used in *58*)
Worked over a number of sts divisible by 13.
1st row *K4, P3, Kb3, P3, rep from * to end.
2nd row *K3, Pb3, K3, P4, rep from * to end.
3rd row *K4, P2, Cr2BP, Kb1, Cr2FK, P2, rep from * to end.

4th row *K2, [Pb1, K1] twice, Pb1, K2, P4, rep from * to end.
5th row *K4, P1, Cr2BP, P1, Kb1, P1, Cr2FK, P1, rep from * to end.
6th row *K1, Pb1, [K2, Pb1] twice, K1, P4, rep from * to end.
7th row *K4, Cr2BP, P1, Kb3, P1, Cr2FK, rep from * to end.
8th row *Pb1, K2, Pb3, K2, Pb1, P4, rep from * to end.
9th row *K4, P2, Cr2BP, Kb1, Cr2FK, P2, rep from * to end.
Rep 4th–9th rows as required.

Single Honeycomb Pattern

An unusual version of a wider and much better known Honeycomb stitch, this can be most effective when used for both welt and central front panel, carrying the eye up the front without the distraction of a break in the continuity.

Worked over a number of sts divisible by 3. If used in a panel 1 more st must be added at the end to finish off the panel edge.
1st row *K2, P1, rep from * to end.
2nd row *K1, P2, rep from * to end.
3rd row Work as for 1st row.
4th row Work as for 2nd row.
5th row *K1, sl next st to CN, hold at front, P1, K1 from CN, rep from * to end.
6th row *P1, K1, P1, rep from * to end.
7th row *K1, P1, K1, rep from * to end.
8th row Work as for 6th row.
9th row Work as for 7th row.
10th row *Sl next st to CN, hold at back, K1, P1 from CN, P1, rep from * to end.

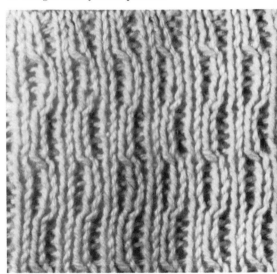

64 Single honeycomb pattern

Trinity Stitch

Trinity stitch, also known in Ireland as Three in One and One in Three, in Scotland as Bramble stitch and in England as Blackberry stitch, has other very close relatives throughout the knitting world.

Worked over a number of sts divisible by 4.
1st row K2, *[K1, P1, K1] all into next st, P3 tog, rep from * to last 2 sts, K2.
2nd and 4th rows P.
3rd row K2, *P3 tog, [K1, P1, K1] all into next st, rep from * to last 2 sts, K2.
Rep these 4 rows as required.

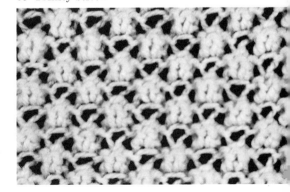

65 Trinity stitch

66 Honeycomb pattern

67 Honeycomb used to form rib

68 Plain lattice pattern

Honeycomb Stitch

Worked with twisted stitches without the use of a cable needle honeycomb can be used as side panels or to form centre panels between larger side patterns, or four stitches side by side can be used to form small ribs or cable-like patterns on their own.

Worked over a number of sts divisible by 4.
1st row *Tw2R, Tw2L, rep from * to end.
2nd row P.
3rd row *Tw2L, Tw2R, rep from * to end.
4th row P.
Rep 1st–4th rows as required.

Plain Lattice

Lattice patterns are a basic necessity of any library of Aran stitches and are not only used in this form but often also to contain different stitch fillings, giving even more texture to the panel.

This panel is worked over 24 stitches and can be seen in use on the side panel of the sweater shown on page 65 (*56*).
Abbreviations used are:
C3R   sl 1 to CN, hold at back, Kb2, P1 from CN.
C3F   sl 2 to CN, hold at front, P1, Kb2 from CN.
C4P   sl 2 to CN, hold at front, Pb2, Pb2 from CN.

1st row P4, Kb4, P8, Kb4, P4.
2nd row K4, Pb4, K8, Pb4, K4.
3rd row P3, C3R, C3L, P6, C3R, C3L, P3.
4th row K3, Pb2, K2, Pb2, K6, Pb2, K2, Pb2, K3.
5th row P2, C3R, P2, C3L, P4, C3R, P2, C3L, P2.
6th row K2 [Pb2, K4] 3 times, Pb2, K2.
7th row P1, C3R, P4, C3L, P2, C3R, P4, C3L, P1.
8th row K1, Pb2, K6, Pb2, K2, Pb2, K6, Pb2, K1.
9th row [C3R, P6, C3L] twice.
10th row Pb2, K8, C4P, K8, Pb2.
11th row [C3L, P6, C3R] twice.
12th row K1, Pb2, K6, Pb2, K2, Pb2, K6, Pb2, K1.
13th row P1, C3L, P4, C3R, P2, C3L, P4, C3R, P1.
14th row K2, [Pb2, K4] 3 times, Pb2, K2.
15th row P2, C3L, P2, C3R, P4, C3L, P2, C3R, P2.
16th row K3, Pb2, K2, Pb2, K6, Pb2, K2, Pb2, K3.
17th row P3, C3L, C3R, P6, C3L, C3R, P3.
18th row K4, C4P, K8, C4P, K4.
Rep 3rd–18th rows as required.

Lace Horseshoe Pattern

Lace patterns are not unknown in Aran knitting and although they may show influence from Shetland they are quite often used in the islanders' own way. This and the following pattern come from the front and the back of one sweater where the difference in shape is connected by the same treatment of stocking stitch pattern accentuated by areas of garter stitch.

The pattern panel is worked over 27 sts.
1st row P5, K5, P7, K5, P5.
2nd and every alt row P.
3rd row P3, P2 tog, K2, yon, K1, yon, K2, P2, P3 tog, P2, K2, yon, K1, yon, K2, P2 tog, P3.
5th row P2, P2 tog, K2, yon, K3, yon, K2, P1, P3 tog, P1, K2, yon, K3, yon, K2, P2 tog, P2.
7th row P1, P2 tog, K2, yon, K5, yon, K2, P3 tog, K2, yon, K5, yon, K2, P2 tog, P1.
8th row P.
Rep 1st–8th rows as required.

Openwork Diamond Pattern

Combined with cables which could be twisted more than these if preferred, or have substitute cable patterns replacing them, the openwork diamonds give a delightful contrast to the more solid areas.

The panel is worked over 39 sts.
The cable pattern is abbreviated to C4, sl next 2 sts to CN, hold at front, K2, K2 from CN.
1st row [P1, K3, P7, K3, P1] K4, P1, K4, rep sts in [ ] once.
2nd row [K1, P5, sl 1, P2 tog, psso, P5, K1], P4, K1, P4, rep sts in [ ] once.
3rd row [P1, K1, yon, K2, P5, K2, yon, K1, P1], K4, P1, K4, rep sts in [ ] once.
4th row [K1, P5, sl 1, P2 tog, psso, P5, K1], P4, K1, P4, rep sts in [ ] once.
5th row [P1, K2, yon, K2, P3, K2, yon, K2, P1], K4, P1, K4, rep sts in [ ] once.
6th row [K1, P5, sl 1, P2 tog, psso, P5, K1], P4, K1, P4, rep sts in [ ] once.
7th row [P1, K3, yon, K5, yon, K3, P1], C4, P1, C4, rep sts in [ ] once.
8th row [K1, P13, K1], P4, K1, P4, rep sts in [ ] once.
9th row [P5, K2, yon, K1, yon, K2, P5], K4, P1, K4, rep sts in [ ] once.
10th row K1, P15, [K1, P4] twice, K1, P15, K1.
11th row [P3, P2 tog, K2, yon, K3, yon, K2, P2 tog, P3], K4, P1, K4, rep sts in [ ] once.
12th row K1, P15, [K1, P4] twice, K1, P15, K1.
13th row [P2, P2 tog, K2, yon, K5, yon, K2, P2 tog, P2], K4, P1, K4, rep sts in [ ] once.
14th row K1, P15, [K1, P4] twice, K1, P15, K1.

69 Lace horseshoe pattern

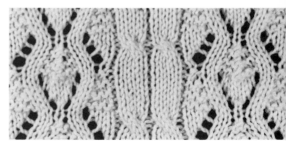

70 Openwork diamond pattern

71

15th row [P1, P2 tog, K2, P7, K2, P2 tog, P1], K4, P1, K4, rep sts in [ ] once.
16th row [K1, P5, sl 1, P2 tog, psso, P5, K1], P4, K1, P4, rep sts in [ ] once.
17th row [P1, K1, yon, K2, P5, K2, yon, K1, P1], K4, P1, K4, rep sts in [ ] once.
18th row [K1, P5, sl 1, P2 tog, psso, P5, K1], P4, K1, P4, rep sts in [ ] once.
19th row [P1, K2, yon, K2, P3, K2, yon, K2, P1], K4, P1, K4, rep sts in [ ] once.
20th row [K1, P5, sl 1, P2 tog, psso, P5, K1], P4, K1, P4, rep sts in [ ] once.
21st row [P1, K3, yon, K5, yon, K3, P1], C4, P1, C4, rep sts in [ ] once.
Rep 8th–21st rows as required.

Half Diamond Pattern

Commercialization has meant that many knitters have lost the opportunity to work many of the larger repeats because of the space the instructions require.

This half diamond repeat can be used to form or to outline centre panels. The reverse panel can be worked by reading these rows from end to beginning and working the reverse cables reading Cr2FK for Cr2BP and Cr2BP for Cr2FK. It is also necessary to work Cr2BKb in place of the Cr2FKb.

The panel is worked over 18 sts.
1st row [Kb1, P1] 5 times, Kb1, [P1, K1] 3 times, P1.
2nd row [K1, P1] 3 times, K1, [Pb1, K1] 5 times, Pb1.
3rd row [Kb1, P1] 3 times, Cr2FKb, [Cr2FK] twice, [P1, K1] 3 times.
4th row [P1, K1] 3 times, [Pb1, K1] twice, Pb2, [K1, Pb1] 3 times.
5th row [Kb1, P1] 3 times, Kb1, [Cr2FK] 3 times, [P1, K1] twice, P1.
6th row [K1, P1] twice, K1, [Pb1, K1] 6 times, Pb1.
7th row [Kb1, P1] 4 times, Cr2FKb, [Cr2FK] twice, [P1, K1] twice.
8th row [P1, K1] twice, [Pb1, K1] twice, Pb2, [K1, Pb1] 4 times.
9th row [Kb1, P1] 4 times, Kb1, [Cr2FK] 3 times, P1, K1, P1.
10th row K1, P1, K1, [Pb1, K1] 7 times, Pb1.
11th row [Kb1, P1] 5 times, Cr2FKb, [Cr2FK] twice, P1, K1.
12th row P1, K1, [Pb1, K1] twice, Pb2, [K1, Pb1] 5 times.
13th row [Kb1, P1] 5 times, Kb1, [Cr2FK] 3 times, P1.
14th row [K1, Pb1] 9 times.
15th row [Kb1, P1] 6 times, Cr2FKb, [Cr2FK] twice.
16th row [Pb1, K1] twice, Pb2, [K1, Pb1] 6 times.

71 Half diamond panel

17th row [Kb1, P1] 6 times, [Cr2BP] 3 times.

18th row [K1, Pb1] 9 times.

19th row [Kb1, P1] 5 times, Kb1, [Cr2BP] 3 times, K1.

20th row P1, K1, [Pb1, K1] twice, Pb2, [K1, Pb1] 5 times.

21st row [Kb1, P1] 5 times, [Cr2BP] 3 times, K1, P1.

22nd row K1, P1, K1, [Pb1, K1] 7 times, Pb1.

23rd row [Kb1, P1] 4 times, Kb1, [Cr2BP] 3 times, K1, P1, K1.

24th row [P1, K1] twice, [Pb1, K1] twice, Pb2, [K1, Pb1] 4 times.

25th row [Kb1, P1] 4 times, [Cr2BP] 3 times, [K1, P1] twice.

26th row [K1, P1] twice, K1, [Pb1, K1] 6 times, Pb1.

27th row [Kb1, P1] 3 times, Kb1, [Cr2BP] 3 times, [K1, P1] twice, K1.

28th row [P1, K1] 3 times, [Pb1, K1] twice, Pb2, [K1, Pb1] 3 times.

29th row [Kb1, P1] 3 times, [Cr2BP] 3 times, [K1, P1] 3 times.

30th row [K1, P1] 3 times, [K1, Pb1] 6 times.

31st row [Kb1, P1] twice, Kb1, [Cr2BP] 3 times, [K1, P1] 3 times, K1.

32nd row [P1, K1] 4 times, [Pb1, K1] twice, Pb2, [K1, Pb1] twice.

33rd row [Kb1, P1] twice, [Cr2BP] 3 times, [K1, P1] 4 times.

34th row [K1, P1] 4 times, [K1, Pb1] 5 times.

35th row Kb1, P1, Kb1, [Cr2BP] 3 times, [K1, P1] 4 times, K1.

36th row [P1, K1] 5 times, [Pb1, K1] twice, Pb2, K1, Pb1.

37th row Kb1, P1, [Cr2BP] 3 times, [K1, P1] 5 times.

38th row [K1, P1] 5 times, K1, [Pb1, K1] 3 times, Pb1.

39th row Kb1, [Cr2BP] 3 times, [K1, P1] 5 times, K1.

40th row [P1, K1] 6 times, [Pb1, K1] twice, Pb2.

41st row Kb1, [Cr2FK] 3 times, [P1, K1] 5 times, P1.

42nd row [K1, P1] 5 times, K1, [Pb1, K1] 3 times, Pb1.

43rd row Kb1, P1, Cr2FKb, [Cr2FK] twice, [P1, K1] 5 times.

44th row [P1, K1] 5 times, [Pb1, K1] twice, Pb2, K1, Pb1.

45th row Kb1, P1, Kb1, [Cr2FK] 3 times, [P1, K1] 4 times, P1.

46th row [K1, P1] 4 times, K1, [Pb1, K1] 4 times, Pb1.

47th row [Kb1, P1] twice, Cr2FKb, [Cr2FK] twice, [P1, K1] 4 times.

48th row [P1, K1] 4 times, [Pb1, K1] twice, Pb2, [K1, Pb1] twice.

49th row [Kb1, P1] twice, Kb1, [Cr2FK] 3 times, [P1, K1] 3 times, P1.

50th row [K1, P1] 3 times, K1, [Pb1, K1] 5 times, Pb1.

Rep 3rd–50th rows as required.

72 Twin lined diamond

Double Twin-lined Diamonds

The neat lines and open spaces of this centre panel make it very useful with side panels of smaller cable repeats. Despite the number of rows to the repeat experienced knitters will know that once the first few rows have been worked the pattern becomes very obvious and is not difficult to follow.

The panel is worked over 30 sts.
1st row [K1, Pb1] twice, K2, Pb1, K1, Pb1, K12, Pb1, K1, Pb1, K2, [Pb1, K1] twice.
2nd row P1, [Cr2FK] twice, P1, [Cr2FK] twice, P10, [Cr2BP] twice, P1, [Cr2BP] twice, P1.
3rd row [K2, Pb1, K1, Pb1], twice, K10, [Pb1, K1, Pb1, K2] twice.
4th row P2, [Cr2FK] twice, P1, [Cr2FK] twice, P8, [Cr2BP] twice, P1, [Cr2BP] twice, P2.
5th and every alt row K all K sts and Pb all Pb sts.
6th row P3, [Cr2FK] twice, P1, [Cr2FK] twice, P6, [Cr2BP] twice, P1, [Cr2BP] twice, P3.
8th row P4, [Cr2FK] twice, P1, [Cr2FK] twice, P4, [Cr2BP] twice, P1, [Cr2BP] twice, P4.
10th row P5, [Cr2FK] twice, P1, [Cr2FK] twice, P2, [Cr2BP] twice, P1, [Cr2BP] twice, P5.
12th row P6, [Cr2FK] twice, P1, [Cr2FK] twice, [Cr2BP] twice, P1, [Cr2BP] twice, P6.
14th row P6, [Cr2BP] twice, P1, [Cr2BP] twice, [Cr2FK] twice, P1, [Cr2FK] twice, P6.
16th row P5, [Cr2BP] twice, P1, [Cr2BP] twice, P2, [Cr2FK] twice, P1, [Cr2FK] twice, P5.
18th row P4, [Cr2BP] twice, P1, [Cr2BP] twice, P4, [Cr2FK] twice, P1, [Cr2FK] twice, P4.
20th row P3, [Cr2BP] twice, P1, [Cr2BP] twice, P6, [Cr2FK] twice, P1, [Cr2FK] twice, P3.
22nd row P2, [Cr2BP] twice, P1, [Cr2BP] twice, P8, [Cr2FK] twice, P1, [Cr2FK] twice, P2.
24th row P1, [Cr2BP] twice, P1, [Cr2BP] twice, P10, [Cr2FK] twice, P1, [Cr2FK] twice, P1.
Rep 1st–24th rows as required.

6 Iceland and the Faroe Islands

73 Icelandic woman by Sigurour
Guomundsson 1833–74. *National
Museum of Iceland*

Of all the northern lands Iceland and the Faroe Islands
seem to have been the most advanced in their hand
knitting. Although under Danish control the influence
would seem to have come from either English or more
probably from German merchants and is thought to have
begun about the middle of the sixteenth century.

By 1624 large numbers of pairs of stockings and mittens
were being exported and by the next century sweaters had
been added to the list of garments sold abroad.

Between the middle of the eighteenth century and the
middle of the nineteenth century exports continued to
grow with men, women and children all making their
contribution, for the children began to knit when they
were eight years old.

Long before knitting brought in payment from exports
the actual wool itself was used in Iceland and the Faroe
Islands as money to buy other goods. Woven into cloth it
was known as 'vadmal' in Iceland and was internationally
accepted as coinage. In the Faroe Islands wool could even
be used to pay fines.

PATTERNED KNITTING

The patterned knitting so well known today is a much
more recent introduction and showed decided
Scandinavian influence until recently, when designing has
been taken very seriously with an eye to producing
Icelandic designs as opposed to copies of Scandinavian
ideas.

Coloured knitting does seem to have been worked to
some extent long before it became really popular
elsewhere and is mentioned as early as 1695 when a two-
coloured item is recorded. However, at that time this may
well have been the exception rather than the rule.

PATTERNS

Even in the matter of patterns Iceland seems to have been
ahead of other countries and two manuscripts of 1776 and
1780 include graph paper designs specifically for coloured
knitting. Some of the designs are reminiscent of many
familiar Scandinavian designs but there are those which
seem to relate to Iceland alone. In particular there is a
ribbon fold pattern which seems to appear nowhere else in
colour and can be seen in very recent designs worked in
the natural browns, cream, rust and black of the sheep.

YARN

Lopi, the soft, almost untwisted yarn so popular today,
was not always used, and it was not until after the coming
of the woollen mills that the possibility arose of using the
yarn in this form, carded but without the firm tightening
twist which it had been usual to give it in spinning.

Both in Iceland and on the Faroe Islands finely spun yarn can be found knitted into lace for stoles and shawls, just as on Unst in the north of Shetland, and also in Russia.

ICELANDIC STITCH PATTERNS

Ribbon Pattern

A more involved border pattern can be worked from this version of the ribbon pattern, simplified in many sweaters today (74 and *fig. 42*).

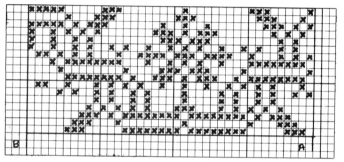

Fig. 42 Chart for ribbon pattern

Two Border Patterns

Simple geometric patterns are ideally suited to the thick yarn which does not need to be heavily patterned to look its best. If used together these two patterns require 24 stitches to each repeat. They could however be used separately with the top border repeating over eight stitches and the lower one over 12 stitches.

The arrowhead border in figs. 44, 76 requires 12 stitches for each repeat and is worked over 12 rows.

More Icelandic designs can be seen on pages 179, 180.

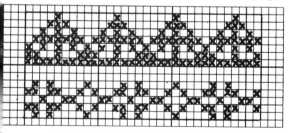

Fig. 43 Chart for two border patterns

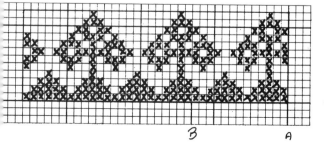

74 Icelandic ribbon pattern

75 Two border patterns

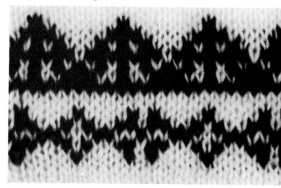

76 Arrowhead border pattern

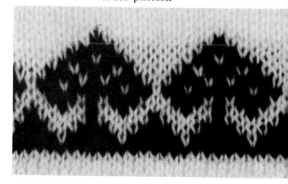

Fig. 44 Chart for arrowhead border

77

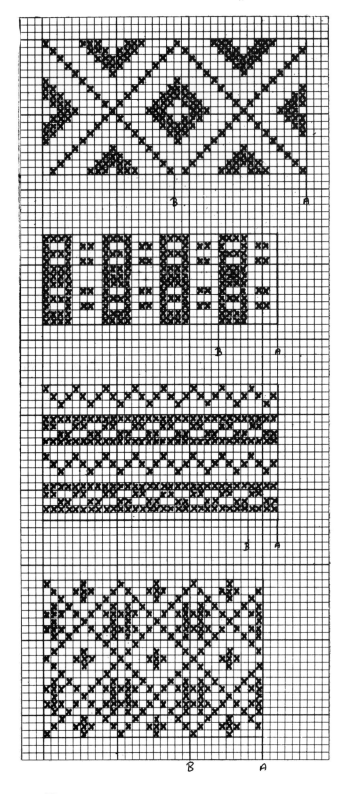

77 Traditional Faroe stitches.
Kunstindustrimuseet, Copenhagen

Fig. 45 Chart for first four patterns

Fig. 46 Chart for second four patterns

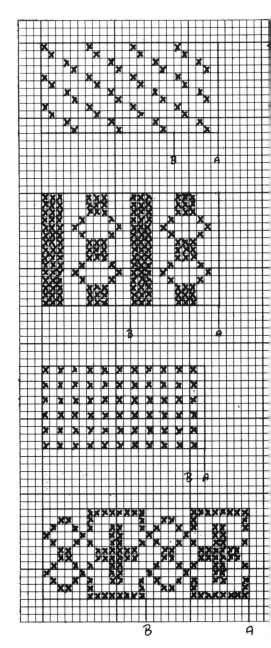

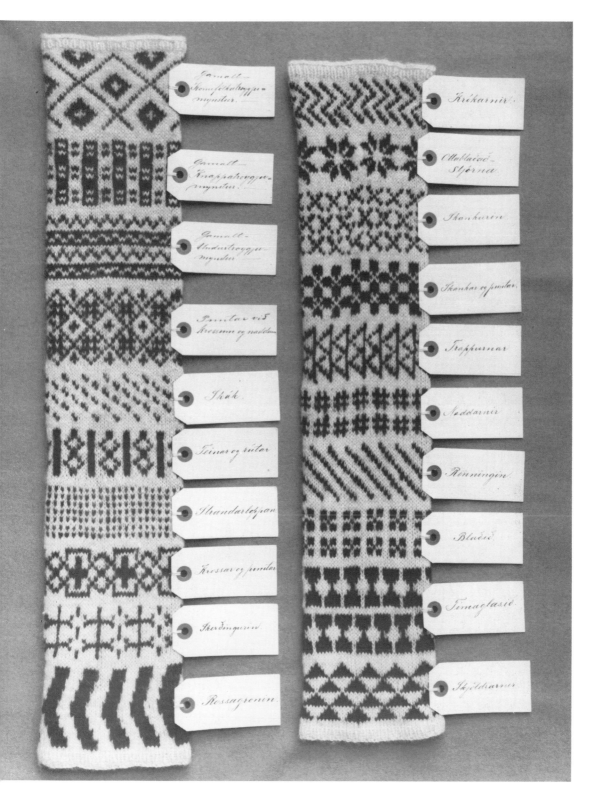

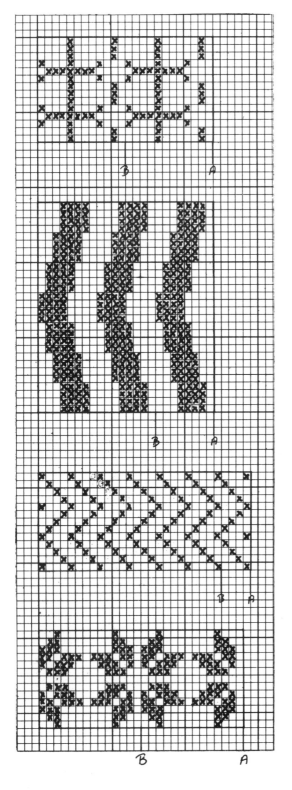

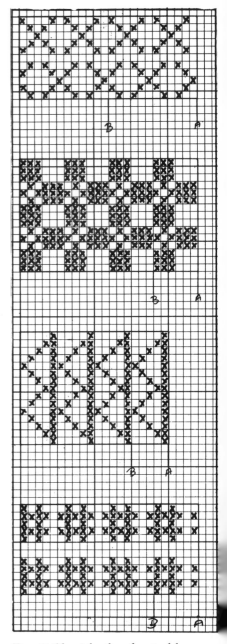

Fig. 48 Chart for fourth set of four patterns

80

LEFT
Fig. 47 Chart for third four patterns

FAROESE PATTERNS

Although similar, in being small geometric designs, the patterns found on the sweaters knitted in the Faroe Islands could never be mistaken for Icelandic patterns, nor are they obviously Scandinavian. They belong essentially to the islands and can be seen to advantage in the photograph (77) which shows the traditional name of each pattern.

It was during the 1920s that the islands were combed for any patterns the knitters could remember using. Each recalled pattern was then knitted in white and yarn of a purplish colour, dyed with the usual *Lecanora tartarea* (a locally collected lichen) and when each had been labelled with its traditional name they were shown in exhibition during 1927 in Copenhagen. There were 30 designs, and they were so outstanding that when Queen Alexandrina saw them she asked that they might be made into a book. In 1932 they were published along with others which had been added to them by that time.

Today these same patterns are used by the islanders for the very attractive designs which they knit.

Used in bands, the patterns are invariably worked on a plain background and are bold and clear, with no shading. Bands may be divided by a narrow pattern but there is a certain restfulness and satisfaction in the repetition of the main band rather than several different patterns each detracting from the others.

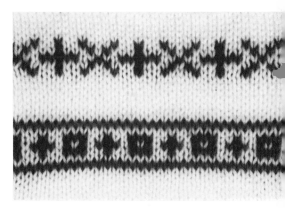

Narrow Bands

The patterns dividing wide bands are very small and like these extend over three, five or seven rows. The lower border repeats over eight stitches and the upper over ten stitches.

78 Two narrow border patterns

Wider Bands

Two bands which are used today but which were not among the early designs are shown here (79). The top band repeats over 12 stitches and the lower band over 20 stitches.

79 (a) LEFT and **(b)** BELOW Two wider border patterns

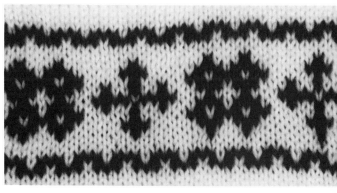

Fig. 49 Chart for last four patterns

Fig. 50 Charts for two narrow
borders

Fig. 51 Charts for two wide borders

7 Sweden

PREVIOUS PAGE
80 Mittens worked in nålbindning.
Nordic Museum, Stockholm

Early fabrics in Sweden, if not woven, were made either in sprang or in a form of single-needle work made by coiling the yarn intricately, before passing the threaded needle through the coils or stitches to hold them in place. It was not until the middle of the seventeenth century that knitting was introduced.

THE INTRODUCTION OF KNITTING

Unlike most countries, the people in the west of Sweden, in the area of Halland, are in no doubts about how knitting was introduced to them or where it came from.

In the middle of the seventeenth century a new Governor was appointed to the area from Denmark and with him came his wife, Magna Brita Cracaus. It was from her that the people learned this new craft, which she in turn had learned from Holland.

KNITTING OF MANY TYPES

Despite the late start, there is a wealth of patterned knitting throughout the country, many areas having outstanding patterns or techniques which are unique. In the west there is knitting which cannot fail to recall the patterns of Shetland, in the east large pattern repeats which are used to contrast red, green and black in a very special way, and in the north small patterns of vivid colour make caps and gloves of endless variation. From Dalarna, the home of so much craft and art, comes the unusual technique of using two ends of yarn even when working one colour, making instant patterning of small, textured designs, ideal for sock tops which are often decorated or for the wrists of mittens where the thicker fabric is warmer and harder wearing.

81 Bjärbo pattern

PATTERNS FROM THE WEST

Bjärbo Pattern

The Bjärbo pattern, striking, old and well designed for knitting with the colour stranded across the back of the work, is still one of the most popular designs in the Halland area.

Traditionally worked in red and blue on a cream background, it is also used in the fashion colours of the moment and may be found in white on grey or light blue, or in white on a background striped amethyst and purple. Knitted round, with the pattern easily visible, the Bjärbo pattern has been used for many years by the expert home knitters of the Handcraft Industries Association. Today the home knitting is cut, again by experts, and made into coats and jackets, fully lined and edged with garter stitch borders often striped in the same colours as the pattern,

B   A

Fig. 52 Chart for Bjärbo pattern

82 Knitters of Halmstad knitting
the Bjärbo pattern. *Britta Johansson*

making a garment of quality as well as of timeless fashion.

The large task of knitting the main section was often shared by two people at once, as demonstrated by Lars Petter Jönsson and his wife, Beata, from Halmstad. This is possible when the work is on several double pointed needles.

Bjärbo Border
The Bjärbo pattern can also be adapted to make it more suitable for a smaller area such as a border.

Tree and Flower Pattern
Another old pattern which was first used on gloves, was originally worked in alternate stripes of two rows red, two rows blue on a light background.

Stocking Patterns
Many good designs can be seen on stockings such as those worn by Lars Jönsson (*83*). This is another pattern which

83 Lars Petter Jönnson and his wife, Beata. *Nordic Museum, Stockholm*

84 Bjärbo border pattern

Fig. 53 Chart for Bjärbo border

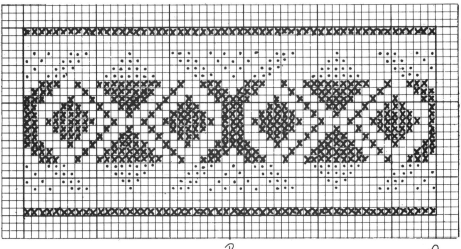

B   A

Fig. 54 Chart for tree and flower pattern

85 Tree and flower pattern

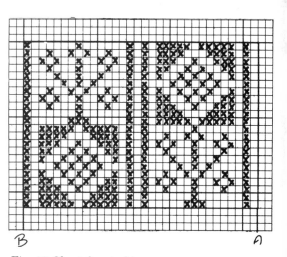

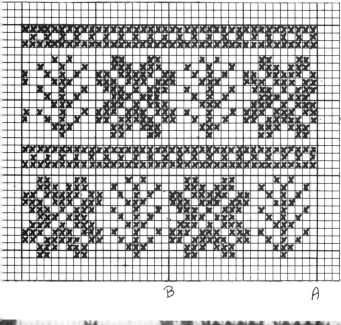

Fig. 55 Chart for stocking pattern

86 Stocking pattern

can be worked in light on dark, dark on light or even with the squares alternated on a self-coloured background.

Gubbamönster

No collection of Scandinavian designs would be complete without a pattern depicting small figures, which look so attractive when knitted. Worked in one colour or two on a light background they are always effective, not difficult to knit, and welcomed by most age groups.

87

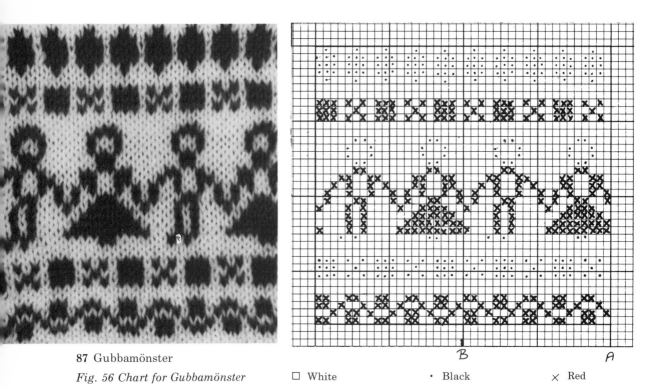

87 Gubbamönster

Fig. 56 Chart for Gubbamönster

☐ White   • Black   ✕ Red

Fig. 57 Chart for flower pattern

88

Flower Patterns

In many Swedish patterns the eight-pointed star, so often used in Norway, becomes softer and is rounded off into flower-like petals. On these mittens it is worked in a very simple pattern with a linking diagonal line joining the flowers into an undeniable all-over pattern.

In the west there is also an enlarged version of this, known as the Laholm flower pattern.

Fig. 58 Chart for Laholm flower pattern

□ White
· Medium
✕ Dark

B   A

88 Flower patterned mittens. *Nordic Museum, Stockholm*

DELSBO PATTERN

In Hälsingland there is a particular use of pattern which is unusual and very striking. At its best three colours are needed and one pattern is most effective in green, red and black or white. The basic design is similar to this one (*89*) where the main pattern is worked in green and red, changing suddenly on a related pattern to one of the colours already used and white, giving vivid contrast. The repeats used are much larger than those found in other areas, and seem always to have been worked with the entire garment in mind.

One example of this type of design in the Nordic Museum in Stockholm has the date knitted into the garment so that there can be no doubt as to when it was knitted, a practice which is of the greatest help to those who follow. This particular pattern, even larger in repeat than the one shown, is dated 1857. Part of the

RIGHT
89 Delsbo pattern

Fig. 59 Chart for Delsbo pattern

☐ Light
· Medium
✕ Dark

90 ℬ 𝒜

charm of these designs is in their colouring. The hand-
dyed green is not too dark and is bright and clear while
the red is incredibly light and vivid, like a flame. Against
either black or white the red contrast is really
remarkable.

PATTERN FROM DALARNA

A drawing made in 1895 by Ottilia Adelborg shows a man
from Holsåkers in Dalarna wearing a homespun jacket
with knitted sleeves. The jacket, in grey, is made
colourful with the addition of the large motif-patterned
sleeves in red with a black pattern.

TECHNIQUE FROM DALARNA

Although the technique of using two strands of yarn, even
for self-coloured work, is not used only in Dalarna, it is
knitted widely in this district, either side of the fabric

90 Man from Holsåkers drawn by
Ottilia Adelborg in 1895. *Nordic
Museum, Stockholm*

being used as the right side. Sock tops worked in this way show the slightly different appearance that it has, and the patterns show very clearly the way in which simple relief patterns are built up.

Two Yarn Casting On

Make a slip knot some way along the strand of yarn from one ball and slip it onto the needle. The distance along the strand will depend on how many stitches are to be cast on. The distance between the knot and the end of the strand is the amount of yarn available for knitting the loops that are cast on, as in the thumb method of casting on. Three times the length of the piece to be cast on will be sufficient.

Make a slip knot 10 cm from the end of the second ball of yarn and slip this onto the needle also.

The two lengths of yarn from the two balls are held in the right hand, as is the needle, with the long tail from the first knot held in the left, unshaded in the diagram.

The third stitch is made by making a loop over the left thumb with the long tail, inserting the needle into it and using the yarn from the first ball to knit a stitch which is retained on the needle.

The fourth stitch is made by making a loop over the left thumb in the same way, inserting the needle tip and knitting a new stitch with the yarn from the second ball.

The number of stitches required is cast on by repeating this alternately using the first then the second balls of yarn until the required number is cast on.

Knitted Rows

The row is knitted in the usual way, except that the two yarns are used alternately, just as on the casting on row.

91 Stocking tops worked in two strand knitting. *Nordic Museum, Stockholm*

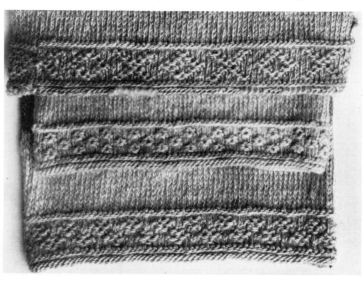

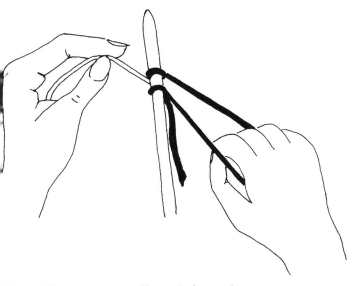

Fig. 60 Two yarns on needle ready for casting on

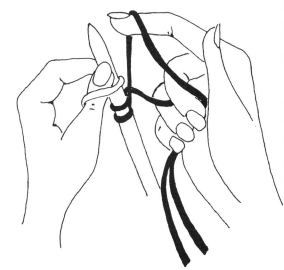

Fig. 61 Working the third stitch

The first ball is used to knit the first stitch, the second ball is used to knit the first stitch, the second ball for the second stitch. To work the third stitch, bring the yarn from the first stitch over the yarn hanging from the second stitch and knit the third stitch.

The fourth stitch is worked by bringing the end from the second stitch over the yarn hanging below the third stitch and knitting the fourth stitch.

Complete the row by alternating the use of the yarns in this way, always passing the yarn to be used over the yarn that has just been used.

Purled Rows
The purl row is worked similarly in as much as the stitches are worked in the usual way and the yarn is

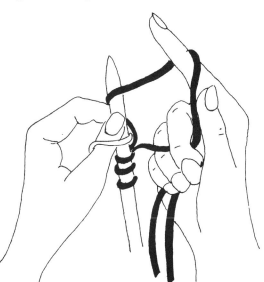

Fig. 62 Working the fourth stitch

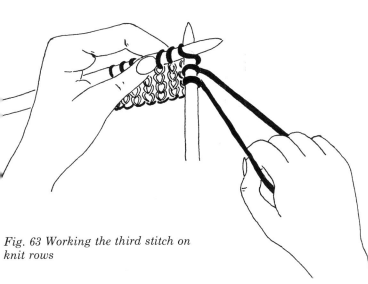

Fig. 63 Working the third stitch on
knit rows

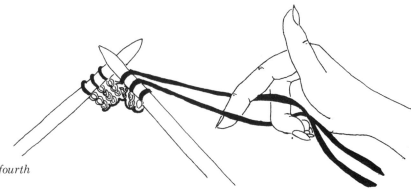

Fig. 64 Preparing to work the fourth stitch on knit rows

alternated as before. The yarn must be taken under the thread from the previous stitch to keep the purled side of the fabric even, with the slanting strands of yarn crossing in the same direction on every row. Keeping the wrong side correct helps to make an even right side.

Working Ridges

Worked with the right side facing, a single ridge is made by taking both strands to the front of the work and working a purl row in the usual way. If the strands are taken back and the next row is also purled the continuity of the stocking stitch can be renewed.

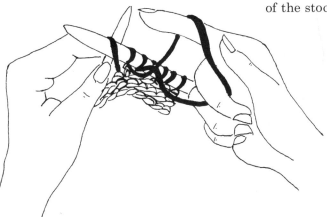

Fig. 65 Lifting the yarn to work the seventh stitch on a purl row

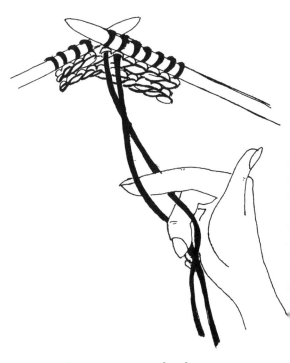

Fig. 66 Taking one yarn under the other on purl side

94

Pattern Unit

The sock top in the centre of photograph 91 shows the single unit on which the other patterns are based. It is worked over two rows and takes the yarn across the front of the work to cover a central stitch on the first row and on the second row covers the front of the stitches to either side of the centre, working the centre stitch to show as a purled stitch on the right side. Worked over an odd number of stitches, it is made as follows:

1st row (right side) Work to 1st before centre st, take yarn used for the st before the last one worked to the front, using this yarn P1. Keeping this yarn at the front use the yarn still at the back to knit the next st, then P1 with the yarn at the front and return it to the back, cont the row as for a K row.

2nd row P to the st before the centre st, take the yarn used for the last st back to the right side, use the yarn still on the wrong side to P the next st, K the next st with the yarn at the right side and leave it there, P the next st with the yarn on the wrong side, bring the yarn from the right side forward to the wrong side and complete the row as for a purl row.

Note: after changing the yarn from the front to the back always check that the correct yarn is picked up to keep the alternating continuity correct.

Diced Pattern

This is formed by the unit already worked, which uses three stitches and is worked over two rows as before, is then alternated and worked over stitches between the first units for the next two rows; then repeat the first two rows.

Worked over a number of sts divisible by 6.

1st row *K3, take the yarn from the st before last to the right side and P1 leaving the yarn forward, K1 using the back yarn, P1 with front yarn and take it back, rep from * to end.

2nd row *Take yarn from st before last st to right side of work and leave it, P1 using wrong-side yarn, K1 using right-side yarn and leave it on right side, P1 using wrong-side yarn, take right-side yarn to wrong side, P3, rep from * to end.

3rd row *Take yarn from st before last st to right side and P1 leaving it at front, K1 with wrong-side yarn, P1 with front yarn and take it back, K3, rep from * to end.

4th row *P3, take yarn from last st to right side leaving it, P1 with wrong side yarn, K1 with right-side yarn leaving it there, P1 with wrong side yarn, take right-side yarn to wrong side, rep from * to end.

5th and 6th rows Work as for 1st and 2nd rows.

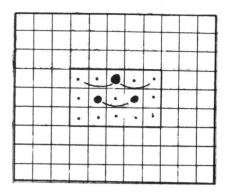

Fig. 67 The position of the strands on the design unit

95

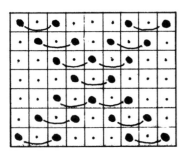

Fig. 68 How the cross is formed

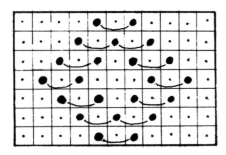

Fig. 69 How the diamond is made

This gives a diced pattern as shown on the middle sock top.

To work a deeper pattern rep 1st–4th rows before completing with 1st and 2nd rows once.

The pattern on the top sock is worked in the same way with only 1 instead of 3 sts between 3 stitch units on the 1st row.

Cross and Diamond Border

Shown on the upper sock top in photograph 92, the cross and diamond are worked in a similar way. The diagram shows how each is constructed so that either can be worked without the other if preferred.

The pattern requires a number of sts divisible by 20.

1st row (right side) *K4, yarn from st before last to front and P1 leaving it forward, using back yarn K1, using front yarn P1 and take it to back, K4, yarn from st before last to front and P1 leaving it forward, using back yarn K1, using front yarn P1 and take it back, K3, yarn from st before last to front and P1 leaving it forward, using back yarn K1, using front yarn P1 and take it back, rep from * to end.

2nd row *P1, yarn from st before last st to right side and K1 leaving it there, using wrong-side yarn P1, using right-side yarn K1 and take it to the wrong side, P1, yarn from st before last to right side and K1 leaving it there, using wrong-side yarn P1, using right-side yarn K1 and take it to wrong side, P4, yarn from st before last to right side and K1 leaving it there, using wrong-side yarn P1, using right-side yarn K1 and leave it there, using wrong-side yarn P1, using right-side yarn K1 and take yarn to wrong side, P3, rep from * to end.

3rd row *K2, yarn from st before last to front and P1 leaving it forward, using back yarn K1, using front yarn P1 and take it back, K1, yarn from st before last to front and P1 leaving it forward, using back yarn K1, using front yarn P1 and take it back, K4, yarn from st before last to front and P1 leaving it forward, using back yarn K1, using front yarn P1 leaving it forward, using back yarn K1, using front yarn P1 and take it back, K2, rep from * to end.

4th row *P3, yarn from st before last to right side and K1 leaving it there, using wrong-side yarn P1, using right-side yarn K1 and take yarn to wrong side, P4, yarn from st before last st to right side and K1 leaving it there, using wrong-side yarn P1, using right-side yarn K1 and take yarn to wrong side, P3, yarn from st before last st to right side and K1 leaving it there, using wrong-side yarn P1, using right-side yarn K1 and take yarn to wrong side, P1, rep from * to end.

5th row Work as for 3rd row.

1 Estonian white lace stole. *For instructions see Chapter 13*

2 Purple and grey Shetland shawl. *For instructions see Chapter 13*

3 Aran sweater (LEFT) and Channel Island guernsey. *For instructions see Chapter 13*

92 Fur-trimmed wristlet in a more complex pattern. *Nordic Museum, Stockholm*

6th row Work as for 2nd row.

7th row Work as for 1st row.

These 7 rows complete the pattern.

A more intricate pattern can be built up as in the wristlet with its fur trimming (*92*).

Coloured Two-strand Knitting

The same method can be used to add coloured edgings to work made in this way.

When the edge is reached one strand is removed and substituted for one coloured strand. The pattern then uses only the stocking stitch pattern but alternate stitches are shown on the right side in the contrast. Where more than one stitch is worked in one colour the original two strands are retained and the coloured strand knitted in as required for the coloured stitches only.

NORTHERN PATTERNS

From Norbotten in the north come geometric patterns which, perhaps because of their bright colours, seem carefree and make the caps and mittens which they adorn fun to knit and fun to wear.

Nothing can seem dull if yellow and green, dotted with white and blue, are worked on a red background.

The patterns are also ideal for use on classic designs that need cheering up and can be worked without undue headaches because of the small pattern repeats which fit easily into any number of stitches.

Both patterns are worked in red, blue and yellow but could be adapted for the colours most suitable. Pattern 1 repeats over 12 stitches and pattern 2 over eight stitches.

97

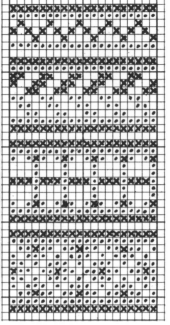

□ Red
• Yellow
× Blue

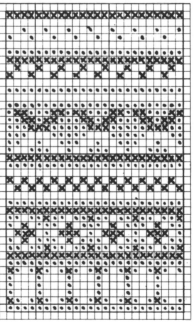

□ Red
• Yellow
× Blue

8 Norway

PREVIOUS PAGE
96 Front of a luskofte from Setesdal. *Norsk Folkesmuseet, Oslo*

As in Sweden, knitting began in Norway at a later date than Britain, Shetland or the south of Europe, probably because the people had other methods of using wool for garment making which proved perfectly satisfactory. Nålbindning, a single-needle technique of working stitches coiled before the insertion of the needle, was widely used in Norway as well as in Sweden, particularly for making woollen mittens, and was preferred to knitting even at the beginning of this century.

EARLY EXAMPLES
Early examples of knitting, but not from Norway, can be found at the Kundstindustrimuseet in Oslo, where there are several silk vests knitted in brocade-type patterns, like the vest possibly worn by Charles I when beheaded. Possibly made in England, but much more likely to have come from Italy, these garments are worth studying because they are beautifully made and are not done justice by a black and white photograph. Shown as they were recently behind gleaming glass and well lit, the light blue, almost turquoise, of the silk seemed to show ideally the purled stitch patterns against the smooth surface of its stocking stitch background. Each garment is finished with gilt embroidery, and, as examples of silk knitting, they are in a different category to the better known silk and gilt jacquard patterned jackets, often edged with plain coloured basket stitch, also from Italy.

LUSKOFTE
The best known Norwegian garment is the ski jacket,

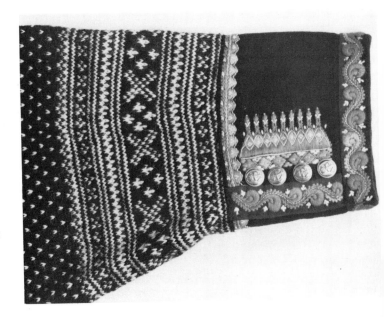

97 Back of Setesdal luskofte. *Norsk Folkesmuseet, Oslo*

98 Detail of embroidered and buttoned cuff. *Norsk Folkesmuseet, Oslo*

luskofte, or, literally, 'lice jacket'. Worked in a firm weatherproof yarn this makes a warm garment worn as an outer covering. The design from Setesdal has been a favourite for many years and has been adapted for the sweater on page 170.

Traditionally only black and white are used for this patterned knitting, colours having been added at a later date. Colour was not missing on this luskofte from Setesdal for the smooth black material used to face neck and cuffs was lavishly embroidered with bright shades of emerald, pink, scarlet, wine and blue, before being finally trimmed with silver clasp and buttons.

Seeding

This pattern is a classic and shows how the main pattern was used across the yoke, with matching but often slightly different deep bands of pattern on sleeve top and above the cuff and lower welt. It also shows how an area of plain seeding was used between other patterns, sometimes, as here, of single stitches, which linked lower and upper patterns. These seeding patterns could be varied and might be three stitches in a triangle or a four-stitch small diamond but were seldom larger than four stitches.

NORWEGIAN TECHNIQUE

The Norwegian technique of knitting round for every type of garment, even if it is to be seamed afterwards as it would be for a jacket, makes for speed of knitting and is not as complicated as it might seem.

Knitted Upwards

All types of garment – sweaters, jackets, cardigans with rounded necks, luskofte, and V-necked pullovers – are knitted in three pieces, one body piece worked without armholes and with the shoulders grafted together, and two sleeves, all knitted from the lower edge upwards.

Pressing

Unless made in a synthetic yarn, each section is pressed under a damp cloth with a warm iron, well blocked out to shape so that the stitches are regular and even, with the ribbing left unpressed.

Cutting Lines

Two lines for the armholes need to be marked, with a contrasting cotton, down the side of the garment to a depth which equals the sleeve top folded in half. If the body is to have an opening, either a full one as for a jacket or a partial one as for a luskofte, it is marked in the same way, always keeping the line straight by following the same stitch from start to finish. Other lines

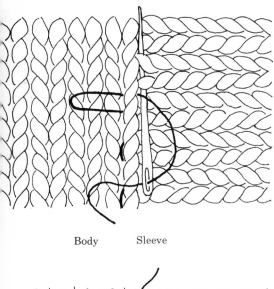

Body   Sleeve

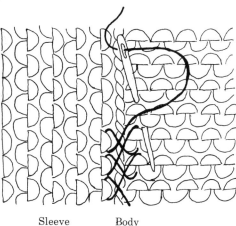

Sleeve   Body

Fig. 72 Norwegian making up

which may need to be marked are those for the neck, either rounded or V-shaped, which will come inside the grafted shoulder stitches.

Stay Stitching

At least two rows of back stitching or machining should be worked with matching cotton or silk immediately inside the cutting line. Some knitters prefer to work four rows, working two rows very close together leaving a gap of not more than a 0.5 cm and working another two rows. This certainly gives a firm line and makes certain that no cut edge slips out of place.

Cutting

Using sharp scissors, cut down the marked cutting lines and cut out a neck section if required.

Stitching

Using a grafting stitch, sew the sleeve top, four rows in from the cast off row, to the stitches on the body inside the last row of stay stitching. The most invisible way is to pick up both strands of one stitch and both strands of the stitch directly opposite, drawing the yarn tight enough so that the edges cannot pull apart, without being so tight that the edges are puckered. Work from underarm to sleeve top and down to the starting point again. Then lay the last four rows of the sleeve top over the cut edge on the wrong side of the work and slip stitch, herringbone or oversew to cover completely the cut edge.

Front Borders

For jackets and cardigans, buttonstrips are added in the same way as the sleeve is attached, stretching the border slightly so that it does not sag below the line of the fronts.

Preparation

Before any pattern is knitted, check which method of finishing is to be used and place the row or round ends to the best advantage. Waistcoats, cardigans and jackets should have the ends starting and finishing at centre front so that they are cut and folded back at the uneven line between the start and finish of the round. Sweaters and garments which are not to be seamed should have the uneven line of pattern exactly on one side.

OTHER PATTERNS

Norwegian patterns are amongst the best known but there is an endless variation. Usually they are worked in two colours with the pattern silhouetted against the background, but some yoked patterns are worked in more than two colours. Again, less traditionally and more for

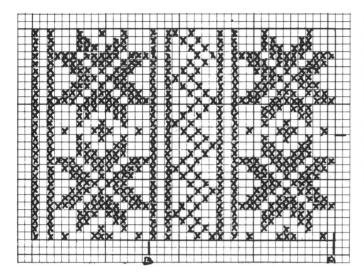

99 Vertical star pattern

Fig. 73 Chart for vertical star pattern

the fashion conscious, there is the possibility of adding additional colour by alternating the colours used for the spot seedings and accentuating a third colour which may be introduced in small quantities in the border or main pattern.

Of all Norwegian patterns perhaps the eight-pointed star remains best known. Used most often in its square form it is also to be found in many more unusual versions in old stocking patterns.

Vertical Star Panel

Once used for stockings, this pattern would lose none of its effect on mittens or even used for a sweater. One complete pattern requires 25 stitches and repeats over 14 rows or rounds.

Half Star Panelled Pattern

Norwegian patterns are worked as Fairisle knitting with the strands carried across the back of the work, easily achieved where there are only a few stitches between colour changes as in this pattern.

The pattern repeats over 20 rows or rounds and uses 28 stitches for each pattern repeat.

Square Patterns

Square patterns make exceptionally useful motifs, either singly on a plain sweater, where they can look most dramatic, or as borders or yokeline panels. Worked as all-over patterns they can often be surprising, forming shapes within repeats that may not have been noticed on the chart. Many of the patterns are snowflake-like in construction, their diagonal lines repeating particularly well as in this version of the Selbu star.

It is worked over 25 stitches and 25 rows.

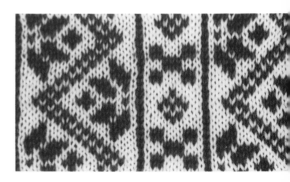

100 Half star pattern

Fig. 74 Chart for half star pattern

Other patterns which are based on Norwegian designs and which are equally attractive worked in only one contrast colour are shown on pages 45, 46 (*27, 28*).

101 Small pattern from Selbu

Fig. 75 Chart for small Selbu pattern

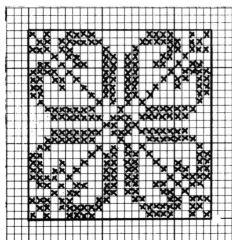

LAPP PATTERNS

From the northern areas of Norway, Sweden and Finland comes the knitting of the Lapps, of a character which is not reflected in the countries around.

Worked in red and blue on cream, occasionally touched with yellow or a paler blue, the simple patterns are easy to knit, often consisting of alternate rows and stitches in the two main contrasting colours.

Diamond Border

A diamond within a diamond, this pattern gives an enormous amount of pattern interest in only a few rows or rounds.

The repeat is only ten stitches, making calculations for caps, mittens and gloves a simple matter. It is worked in red and blue on cream.

Fig. 76 Chart for Lapp diamond border

□ Cream
· Blue
× Red

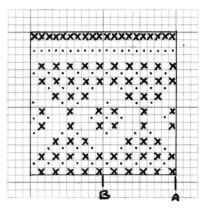

102 Diamond border from Lapland

Three-Colour Pattern

The use of three colours makes this pattern a little different from many of the Lapp patterns; in this case yellow is added to the traditional blue, red and cream.

The repeat is again over ten stitches.

Cross and Wave Border

A particularly unusual border pattern uses a strong waved pattern and the cross which has been used before. To make it into a repeating all-over pattern repeat the crosses only after the 26 row pattern has been worked once.

The crosses repeat over ten stitches but the waved border is an eight-stitch repeat.

Fig. 77 Chart for three-colour pattern

□ Cream
╱ Yellow
· Red
× Blue

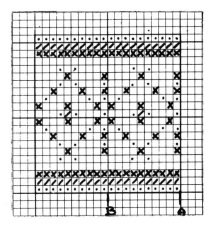

103 Three-coloured border

104 Wave and cross pattern

□ Cream
· Blue
× Red

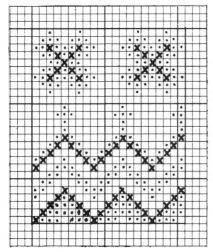

Fig. 78 Chart for wave and cross pattern

Many-striped Pattern

This many-tiered pattern using small geometric shapes almost links Shetland with Finland for the small diamonds are certainly found in Shetland and the bold crosses begin to echo notes of the bolder eastern designs; but the colouring of red and blue is essentially that of the

105 Many-striped pattern

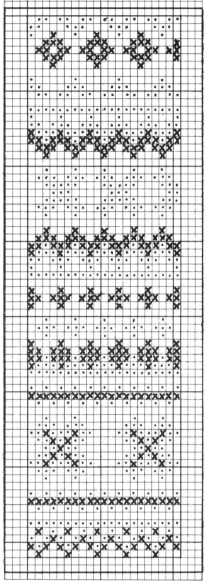

Fig. 79 Chart for many-striped Lapp pattern

Lapps. It makes a charming mitten pattern worked in rounds or can be worked on the back only if working in rows. Basically an interesting pattern, it could be used for borders, yokes or as a repeating all-over pattern.

The main cross repeats over 12 stitches, but note that the entire pattern does not repeat across; most of the shapes repeat on four stitches but the middle-sized cross takes eight, therefore requiring 24 stitches to a complete repeat.

Another Lapp pattern can be found in the Lapp mitten instruction on page 180.

LAPP TECHNIQUE

Most Lapp mittens begin either with ribbing or with a slanting pattern which is used throughout the area and also in Finland. Effective and with many possibilities as a pattern dividing or accentuating line, it is usually worked with one colour and cream, possibly alternating the colours used in the rest of the design.

It is worked in very much the same way as the wrong side of the Swedish two-end knitting, but seems only to be used as an edging, never for the complete mitten.

Use two colours on an even number of sts with A, cream and B, contrast.
1st row (right side) P1A, leave A at front and P1B, drop B and *lift A over it, P1A, drop A and lift B over it, P1B, drop B, rep from * to end.
2nd row Using A, P.
Rep rows 1 and 2 substituting B for other colours if preferred. These instructions are for rows. If working round the second round must be worked using A as a K round.

106 Detail of Lapp edging

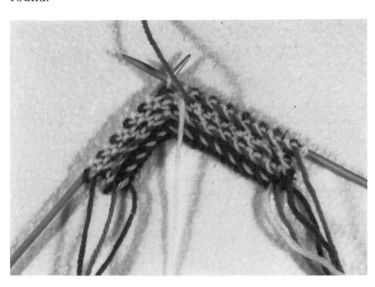

9 Central Europe

107 Man with stirring spoon by Kaspar Kaltenmoser. *Staatiche Graphische Sammlung, Munchen*

Knitting spread quickly to central Europe and the transition from two needles probably used for the pre-twelfth-century knitting to knitting round with four or more double-pointed needles, is recorded in the well known 'Knitting Madonna' painted by Master Bertram of Munich around 1390, and now in the Kunsthall, Hamburg although formerly in the convent of the Benedictine Sisters in Buxtehuder.

By the Middle Ages knitting had become a more serious business and as its commercial potential was realized it was organized into Guilds by men for men, only becoming a domestic occupation again at a later date.

PATTERNED STOCKINGS

In Austria and Bavaria, knitted stockings, particularly for men, were part of the national costume from the eighteenth century, and are mentioned in *Steirisches Trachtenbuch* by B. Geramb as dating from at least 1780.

Knitted in cream wool, these patterned stockings were often very elaborate with patterns which take the stocking shape, twisting and twining in panels over the entire surface or beginning from a twisted, almost sculptured clock, and swelling out into patterned panels, assisting in the excellent shaping of the stocking.

From the Tirol come stockings which are panelled in plaited stitches down the back of the leg and in an additional pattern from the clock above the ankle.

Simpler stockings were often found, mostly worked in twisted rib above a mid-calf clock, as on the stockings of the country gentleman, stirring spoon in hand, drawn by Kaspar Kaltenmoser. The variations obtainable with these patterns seem endless and are added to by the use of relief stitches as side panels.

WAISTCOATS

The plaited patterns, alone or teamed with relief stitches, are widely used for jackets and waistcoats, with or without sleeves. A sleeveless version can be knitted from the instructions given on page 158.

CROSSED STITCHES

Many of the travelling stitch patterns use stitches which move only one position at a time, unlike cable patterns where several stitches are usually involved in the move. This allows a twist stitch technique to be used, omitting the use of a cable needle, which can make the patterns much quicker to work.

This meant that when stockings were worked in the round only eight abbreviations were used to cover all possible moves, four when the knit or purl stitches were

108 Tirolean sock, *Tiroler Volkskunstmuseum, Innsbruck*

untwisted and four when the knit or purl stitches were worked through the back of the loop. In working on two needles this does mean additional abbreviations for the movement of stitches on wrong-side rows. Not all patterns, however, use all the methods of crossing in one pattern.

CHARTING

So that patterns can be seen at a glance without the complication of words which can take up a great deal of space, they are often shown in chart form. These are usually printed as if the right side of the work is facing the knitter, allowing her to choose whether they are worked round or worked on two needles; the same chart can be used for both. The advantage can be seen in the following example.

Chart B shows a simple pattern, knitted in *109*. In words it might be written as follows:

Worked on 2 needles over a panel of 4 sts.
1st row P1, Kb2, P1.
2nd row K1, Pb2, K1.
3rd row P1, Cr2LK by passing needle behind 1st st and K 2nd st tbl then K 1st st tbl before slipping both off left needle, P1.
4th row Work as for 2nd row.
5th and 6th rows Work as for 1st and 2nd rows.
Rep 1st–6th rows as required.

The alternative twist or cross would be shown by using a different symbol on the chart, as in fig. 80C.

In the following few examples of these patterns the chart and instructions for working on two needles will both be given.

Fig. 80 Charts for (A) symbols; (B) left sloping simple twist pattern; (C) right sloping simple twist pattern

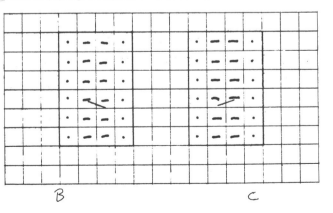

B   C

109 Simple twist

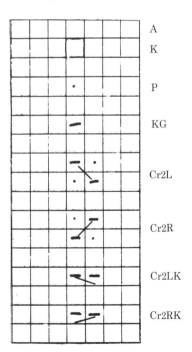

	A
K	K
P	P
KG	KG
Cr2L	Cr2L
Cr2R	Cr2R
Cr2LK	Cr2LK
Cr2RK	Cr2RK

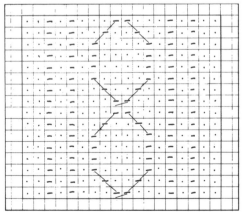

Symbols

The symbols used in these charts are shown in fig. 80A, which gives the stitches as they appear on the right side of the knitting.

If you are working from the chart in rows, right-side rows will read from right to left and wrong-side rows from left to right. If a stitch on the chart shows as knit on a wrong-side row it must be purled. All stitches which appear on the right side as twisted knit stitches must be purled through the back of the stitch on the wrong side.

The abbreviations used are as follows:

Cr2L   pass needle behind 1st st, P 2nd st then Kb 1st st and slip both sts off left needle tog.

Cr2R   pass needle in front of 1st st, Kb 2nd st then P 1st st and slip both sts off left needle tog.

Cr2LK   pass needle behind 1st st, Kb 2nd st then Kb 1st st and slip both sts off left needle tog.

Cr2RK   pass needle in front of 1st st, Kb 2nd st then Kb 1st st and slip both sts off left needle tog.

On the wrong side they must be worked in a different way.

Each of the previous abbreviations is given a wrong side abbreviation which uses the right side abbreviation with a W in front because of course they will look the same when the right side is facing. They are:

WCr2L   pass needle behind 1st st, Pb 2nd st then K 1st st before slipping both sts off left needle tog.

WCr2R   pass needle in front of 1st st, K 2nd st then Pb 1st st before slipping both sts off left needle tog.

WCr2LK   pass needle behind 1st st, Pb 2nd st, then Pb 1st st before slipping both sts off left needle tog.

WCr2RK   pass needle in front of 1st st, Pb 2nd st then Pb 1st st before slipping both sts off left needle tog.

110 Simple round twist

Fig. 81 Chart for single round cross

Single Round Cross

This very simple pattern repeats over eight rows and is accentuated by twin, twisted stitch lines up either side.

Worked over a panel of 18 sts.

1st row (right side) P2, [Kb1, P1] twice, P2, Cr2RK, P2, [P1, Kb1] twice, P2.

2nd row K2, [Pb1, K1] twice, K1, WCr2L, WCr2R, K2, [Pb1, K1] twice, K1.

3rd row P2, [Kb1, P1] twice, Cr2R, P2, Cr2L, [P1, Kb1] twice, P2.

4th row K2, [Pb1, K1] twice, Pb1, K4, Pb1, [K1, Pb1] twice, K2.

5th row P2, [Kb1, P1] 3 times, P2, [P1, Kb1] 3 times, P2.

6th row Work as for 4th row.

7th row P2, [Kb1, P1] twice, Cr2L, P2, Cr2R, P1, [Kb1, P1] twice, P1.

8th row K2, [Pb1, K1] twice, K1, WCr2R, WCr2L, K1, [K1, Pb1] twice, K2.
Rep 1st–8th rows as required.

Intertwined Chains

Links of crossed stitches within other crossed stitches always give the fabric added texture and make a pattern worth knitting.

The panel is worked with single twisted lines down either side. It is worked over 20 sts and repeats over 24 rows.

1st row (right side) P2, Kb1, P6, Cr2RK, P6, Kb1, P2.
2nd row K2, Pb1, K5, WCr2LK, WCr2RK, K5, Pb1, K2.
3rd row P2, Kb1, P4, Cr2R, Kb2, Cr2L, P4, Kb1, P2.
4th row K2, Pb1, K4, Pb1, K1, Pb2, K1, Pb1, K4, Pb1, K2.
5th row P2, Kb1, P4, Kb1, P1, Kb2, P1, Kb1, P4, Kb1, P2.
6th row Work as for 4th row.
7th row P2, Kb1, P4, Cr2L, Kb2, Cr2R, P4, Kb1, P2.
8th row K2, Pb1, K5, WCr2R, WCr2L, K5, Pb1, K2.
9th row Work as for 1st row.
10th row Work as for 2nd row.
11th row Work as for 3rd row.
12th row K2, Pb1, K3, WCr2L, K1, Pb2, K1, WCr2R, K3, Pb1, K2.
13th row P2, Kb1, P2, Cr2R, P1, Cr2RK, Cr2LK, P1, Cr2L, P2, Kb1, P2.
14th row K2, Pb1, K1, WCr2L, K1, WCr2L, WCr2RK, WCr2R, K1, WCr2R, K1, Pb1, K2.
15th row P2, [Kb1, P1] twice, Cr2R, P1, Kb2, P1, Cr2L, [P1, Kb1] twice, P2.
16th row K2, Pb1, K1, Pb1, WCr2L, K2, WCr2RK, K2, WCr2R, Pb1, K1, Pb1, K2.
17th row P2, Kb1, P1, Cr2LK, P3, Kb2, P3, Cr2RK, P1, Kb1, P2.
18th row K2, Pb1, K1, Pb1, WCr2R, K2, WCr2RK, K2, WCr2L, Pb1, K1, Pb1, K2.
19th row P2, [Kb1, P1] twice, Cr2L, P1, Kb2, P1, Cr2R, [P1, Kb1] twice.
20th row K2, Pb1, K1, WCr2R, K1, WCr2R, WCr2RK, WCr2L, K1, WCr2L, K1, Pb 1, K2.
21st row P2, Kb1, P2, Cr2L, P1, Cr2L, Cr2R, P1, Cr2R, P2, Kb1, P2.
22nd row K2, Pb1, K3, WCr2R, K1, Pb2, K1, WCr2L, K3, Pb1, K2.
23rd row Work as for 7th row.
24th row Work as for 8th row.
Rep 1st–24th rows as required.

Plaited Half-diamond Panel

This panel introduces two stitches that are side by side

111 Intertwined chains

Fig. 82 Chart for intertwined chains

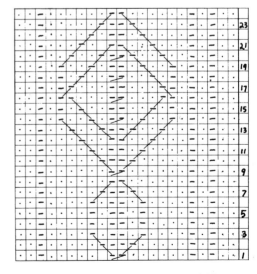

113

112 Plaited half diamond

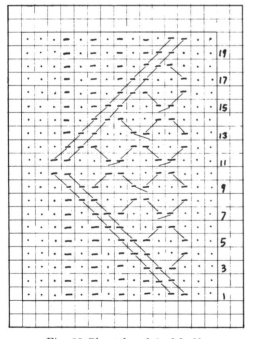

Fig. 83 Chart for plaited half diamond

and are travelled sideways. This needs additional abbreviations and also requires the use of a cable needle.

The additional abbreviations used are as follows:

C3L   sl next 2 sts to CN, hold at front (right side), Kb1, Kb2 from CN.

C3R   sl next st to CN, hold at back (wrong side), Kb2, Kb1 from CN.

WC3L   sl next st to CN, hold at front (wrong side), Pb2, K1 from CN.

WC3R   sl next 2 sts to CN, hold at right side, K1, Pb2 from CN.

The panel is worked over 15 sts.

1st row (right side), P2, Kb2, [P1, Kb1] 4 times, P3.
2nd row K3, [Pb1, K1] 3 times, Pb1, WC3L, K2.
3rd row P3, C3L, [P1, Kb1] 3 times, P3.
4th row K3, [Pb1, K1] twice, Pb1, WC3L, WCr2R, K2.
5th row P2, Kb1, P2, C3L, [P1, Kb1] twice, P3.
6th row K3, Pb1, K1, Pb1, WC3L, WCr2R, WCr2L, K2.
7th row P3, Cr2RK, P2, C3L, P1, Kb1, P3.
8th row K3, Pb1, WC3L, WCr2R, WCr2L, WC2R, K2.
9th row P2, Kb1, P2, Cr2LK, P2, C3L, P3.
10th row K2, WC3L, [WCr2R, WCr2L] twice, K2.
11th row P3, [Cr2RK, P2] twice, Kb2, P2.
12th row K2, WC3R, [WCr2L, WCr2R] twice, K2.
13th row P2, Kb1, P2, Cr2LK, P2, C3R, P3.
14th row K3, Pb1, WC3R, WCr2L, WCr2R, WCr2L, K2.
15th row P3, Cr2RK, P2, C3R, P1, Kb1, P3.
16th row K3, Pb1, K1, Pb1, WC3R, WCr2L, WCr2R, K2.
17th row P2, Kb1, P2, C3R, [P1, Kb1] twice, P3.
18th row K3, [Pb1, K1] twice, Pb1, WC3R, WCr2L, K2.
19th row P3, C3R, [P1, Kb1] 3 times, P3.
20th row K3, [Pb1, K1] 3 times, Pb1, WC3R, K2.
Rep 1st–20th rows as required.

Tirolean Stocking Clock

The more complex patterns on this type of stocking can be charted in the same way as the simpler patterns and are often far easier to work than might be imagined.

On the last row before starting to work from the chart it is necessary to increase one stitch in the rib which will be in the centre so that two stitches can be knitted in the centre on the first row of the chart without spoiling the continuity of the rib on either side. Additional abbreviations are required when the clock instructions are written fully:

C3RP   sl next st to CN, hold at wrong side, Kb2, P1 from CN.

C3LP   sl 2 to CN, hold on right side, P1, Kb2 from CN.

WC3RP sl next 2 sts to CN, hold on right side, Pb1, Pb2 from CN.

WC3LP   sl next st to CN, hold on wrong side, Pb2, Pb1
        from CN.

The pattern is shown worked over 26 sts.

1st row [Kb1, P1] 6 times, Kb2, [P1, Kb1] 6 times.

2nd row [Pb1, K1] 6 times, WCr2R, [K1, Pb1] 6 times.

3rd row [Kb1, P1] 5 times, Kb1, Cr2RK, Cr2LK, Kb1, [P1, Kb1] 5 times.

4th row [Pb1, K1] 5 times, WC3L, WC3R, [K1, Pb1] 5 times.

5th row [Kb1, P1] 4 times, Kb1, C3R, P2, C3L, Kb1, [P1, Kb1] 4 times.

6th row [Pb1, K1] 4 times, WC3L, WCr2R, WCr2L, WC3R, [K1, Pb1] 4 times.

7th row [Kb1, P1] 3 times, Kb1, C3R, P2, Cr2RK, P2, C3L, Kb1, [P1, Kb1] 3 times.

8th row [Pb1, K1] 3 times, WC3L, [WCr2R, WCr2L] twice, WC3R, [K1, Pb1] 3 times.

9th row [Kb1, P1] twice, Kb1, C3R, [P2, Cr2LK] twice, P2, C3L, Kb1, [P1, Kb1] twice.

10th row [Pb1, K1] twice, WC3L, [WCr2R, WCr2L] 3 times, WC3R, [K1, Pb1] twice.

11th row [Kb1, P1] twice, Kb2, [P2, Cr2RK] 3 times, P2, Kb2, [P1, Kb1] twice.

12th row [Pb1, K1] twice, WC3RP, [WCr2L, WCr2R] 3 times, WC3LP, [K1, Pb1] twice.

13th row Kb1, P1, Kb1, Cr2RK, C3LP, [P2, Cr2LK] twice, P2, C3RP, Cr2LK, Kb1, P1, Kb1.

14th row Pb1, K1, WC3L, K1, WC3R, [WCr2L, WCr2R] twice, WC3L, K1, WC3R, K1, Pb1.

15th row Kb1, P1, Kb2, P3, C3LP, P2, Cr2RK, P2, C3RP, P3, Kb2, P1, Kb1.

16th row Pb1, K1, Pb2, K4, WC3R, WCr2L, WCr2R, WC3L, K4, Pb2, K1, Pb1.

17th row Kb1, P1, C3L, P4, C3LP, P2, C3RP, P4, C3R, P1, Kb1.

18th row Pb1, K1, Pb1, WC3R, K4, WC3R, WC3L, K4, WC3L, Pb1, K1, Pb1.

19th row [Kb1, P1] twice, C3L, P4, Cr2L, Cr2RK, P4, C3R, [P1, Kb1] twice.

20th row [Pb1, K1] twice, Pb1, WC3RP, K4, WCr2RK, K4, WC3LP, Pb1, [K1, Pb1] twice.

21st row [Kb1, P1] 3 times, C3L, P3, Cr2RK, P3, C3R, [P1, Kb1] 3 times.

22nd row [Pb1, K1] 3 times, Pb1, WC3RP, K2, WCr2RK, K2, WC3LP, Pb1, [K1, Pb1] 3 times.

23rd row [Kb1, P1] 4 times C3L, P1, Cr2RK, P1, C3R, [P1, Kb1] 3 times.

24th row [Pb1, K1] 4 times, Pb1, WC3RP, WCr2RK, WC3LP, Pb1, [K1, Pb1] 4 times.

25th row [Kb1, P1] 5 times, C3L, C3R, [P1, Kb1] 5 times.

26th row [Pb1, K1] 5 times, Pb1, WCr2LK, WCr2RK, Pb1,

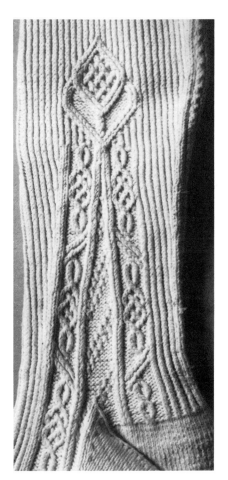

113 Sock clock. *Tiroler Volkskunstmuseum, Innsbruck*

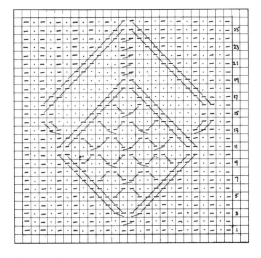

Fig. 84 Chart for stocking clock

ABOVE
114 Tirolean pleated leg coverings.
*Tiroler Volkskunstmuseum,
Innsbruck*

115 Tirolean tufted hat. *Tiroler
Volkskunstmuseum, Innsbruck*

[K1, Pb1] 5 times.
These rows complete the clock.

CHANGING TRENDS

Even in traditional knitting fashions change and
throughout the years many techniques have been in use
which, possibly only temporarily, are out of use.

Tirolean Warmth

Wool holds warmth and the knitters of the Tirol had two
very special methods of using this in their knitting.

One method of gaining extra protection was in the use
of looped knitting for a double knitted hat. Two surfaces
are worked, a top and a lining, much as in a Swedish cap,
but shaped almost conically. To this knitted surface on
the outer side are added loops or strands of yarn much as
a fringe is added to a scarf. Worked densely all over the
surface, it adds considerably to the bulk of the hat.

Another warming idea from the same region is long,
almost straight, cream-coloured leg warmers. Worked
about three times longer than the legs they are to cover,
they are pleated or folded into tucks for wearing and can
be seen in *114* beneath the edge of the skirt. Knitted in
stocking stitch, they are usually made in natural cream-
coloured wool.

Bead Knitting

By the eighteenth century knitting was a pastime in many
countries and was often worked in dainty stitch patterns.
Many patterns were decorated with glass beads, either all

116

116 Beaded cap. *National Museum of Switzerland, Zurich*

over the fabric, known as beaded knitting, and often used for the making of purses, or less solidly, as for the baby's bonnet, which is better described as knitting with beads. This is a technique which is not always in fashion but which is often revived, particularly for the decoration of evening wear.

Beaded Knitting

In patterns where there are beads all over the fabric, it is the bead pattern which shows, not the knitting, and it has to be worked in a special way, the beads being arranged in pattern first and threaded onto the yarn in reverse order so that each bead will automatically be knitted into its correct position.

Knitting with Beads

The technique used by knitters to accentuate a pattern or work a bead border is different and, although the beads still have to be threaded onto the yarn, they are usually of one type, so the order of threading is not as important as when different colours have to form a picture.

The simplest way of working a pattern is to slip a bead in front of a stitch that is not knitted, leaving it there by taking the yarn back into position to work the next stitch.

Threading the Yarn

If there is an art in knitting with beads it is the way in which the beads are placed onto the knitting yarn. It is not possible to thread small beads directly onto yarn because any needle which will take the yarn will not pass through the bead.

The answer is shown in fig. 85, where a fine needle

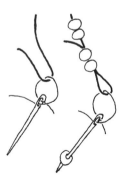

Fig. 85 Threading beads onto yarn

117

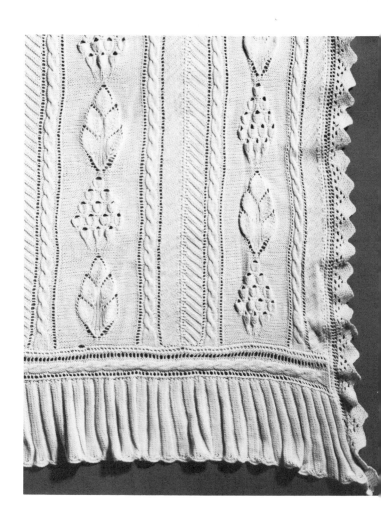

117 Bedspread with panels. *The Museum of History, Berne*

threaded with sewing cotton is looped through the eye so that it can in turn have the yarn placed in the doubled thread. The needle can then pass through the bead onto the cotton and onto the doubled end of yarn and so down the strand, until enough beads are on the ball to start knitting.

White Knitting

With the introduction of white cotton yarn onto the market during the eighteenth century there was a boom in domestic knitting with items of many different types being worked.

One of the most fascinating developments was the making of bedspreads, many of which are still in existence. This example (*117*) was worked in Switzerland and is now in the Museum of History in Berne.

Knitted Bedspreads

One of the advantages of knitting bedspreads was that

they were usually made in small sections, panels, squares or hexagons, and so could easily be accommodated in a work box, only becoming sizable when ready for completion.

Again the ingenuity of the knitter and the flexibility and potential of knitting are well illustrated, with patterns of brocade-like fabrics, lace designs, shapes accentuated with bobbles, rope-inspired panels of cable, and embossed patterns with many different stitch textures all holding their place.

Although bedspreads are to be found in a wide variety of countries including Britain and America, a great many come from central Europe and are recorded in the inexpensive knitting books which abounded from about 1840, many of which were printed in Germany.

Fan Patterned Bedspread

All popular patterns can be found in many different variations, some more successful than others. The fan shape was often used, perhaps because it is so different from the square, but the variation shown here (118) with its openwork edging to each fan and its nicely textured surface, is a particularly good example.

Just as suitable for today as when first knitted, this fan pattern has many possibilities when worked in colour, shading the rows of fans or alternating dark with light. The construction of the fan with its contrasting ridges makes the entire shape possible because each part is in fact simply a triangle. When sewn together, with some degree of precision, the ridges spread open forming a curve which is unexpected and needs correct making up to enhance.

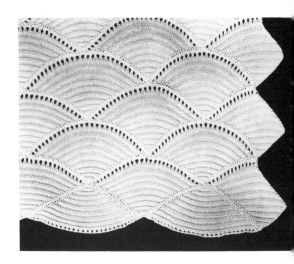

118 Fan patterned bedspread. *The National Museum of Switzerland, Zurich*

Complete Fan

Cast on 55 sts.
1st row K1, *yon, K2 tog, rep from * to end.
2nd row P.
3rd row P1, P2 tog, P to end of row.
4th row K1, K2 tog, K to end of row.
5th row P1, P2 tog, P to end of row.
Rep 3rd, 4th and 5th rows until 3 sts rem.
Cast off.

Right Half Fan

Cast on 29 sts.
1st and 2nd rows Work as for complete fan.
3rd row P1, inc in next st, P to end.
4th row K1, K2 tog, K to end.
5th row P1, inc in next st, P to end.
6th row P1, P2 tog, P to end.
7th row K1, inc in next st, K to end.
8th row P1, P2 tog, P to end.

119 Square pattern bedspread. *The National Museum of Switzerland, Zurich*

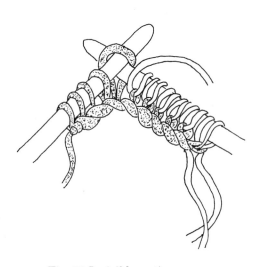

Fig. 86 Invisible casting on

Rep last 6 rows 3 times more then rows 3, 4, 5 and 6 once.
Keeping ridge pattern correct dec 1 st at each side on alt rows until 3 sts rem.
Cast off.

Left Half Fan
Cast on 29 sts.
Work as for right half fan, reversing shaping of first section and completing the second part in the same way.

Square Patterns
A well made (both well knitted and well made up) bedspread in one of the old square-based designs is both a work of art and often fascinating as well in the shapes within shapes which appear as the textures build patterns of their own.

Many patterns use a square worked diagonally, with a large embossed leaf motif in the centre. When four of these squares are sewn together they make a larger square as in the English garden plot pattern or in this Swiss pattern with its delightful use of texture.

Patterns need not be as large as this and a quite simple square worked in ridges, joined so that four squares accentuate the meeting of the ridges and contrasting lights that are formed, is still used in one of the beautiful rooms in Craigievar Castle in Aberdeenshire.

Small Square
Cast on 1 st.
1st row Inc twice into 1st st. (3 sts).
2nd row P.
3rd row K1, M1, K1, M1, K1.
4th row P.
5th row K1, M1, K to last st, M1, K1.
6th row K.
7th row P1, M1, P to last st, M1, P1.
8th row K.
9th row P1, M1, P to last st, M1, P1.
10th row K.
11th row K1, M1, K to last st, M1, K1.
12th row P.
13th row K1, M1, K to last st, M1, K1.
14th row P.
15th row K1, M1, K to last st, M1, K1.
Cont. in this way inc at each end of every alt row until there are 4 purl stripes showing on the right side.
Work 5 rows in st st beg with a K row inc 1 st at each end of next 2 K rows only.
P 1 row.
Work 4 rows more in st st dec 1 st at each end of K rows.
Now cont the stripe sequence as before dec 1 st at each end of every right side row until 3 sts rem.
Cast off.

4 Turkish stocking

5 Grey-green modern Shetland sweater, designed, knitted and worn by Mrs Annabel Bray of Sandwick, Shetland

6 Icelandic sweater in natural colours. *For instructions see Chapter 13*

7 Norwegian sweater. *For instructions see Chapter 13*

TECHNIQUES

In a region with so many different ways of life and with a history of knitting that has covered so many centuries there are many techniques which are not necessarily found in other areas. Finish is of particular importance and methods of casting on and off can improve the appearance of the finished work.

Invisible Casting On

This is worked on K1, P1 rib by casting on using a contrasting coloured yarn, removed afterwards, leaving a neatly rounded edge with a finished, rolled look, rather than a straight rather hard edge which does not add to the quality of the garment.

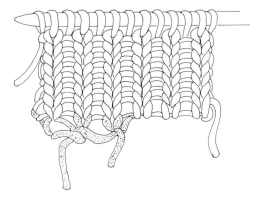

Fig. 87 Removing contrast yarn

BELOW
Fig. 88 Invisible casting off

Using a contrast yarn cast on half the required number of sts, plus 1 extra st.
Using the correct yarn begin the actual ribbed edge:
1st row (right side) K1, *yon, K1, rep from * to end.
2nd row Yarn forward, sl 1, *yarn back, K1, yarn forward, sl 1, rep from * to end.
3rd row K1, *yarn forward, sl 1, yarn back, K1, rep from * to end.
4th and 5th rows Rep 2nd and 3rd rows.
6th row P1, *K1, P1, rep from * to end.
7th row K1, *P1, K1, rep from * to end.
Continue in rib for the required length. Remove the contrast yarn when the part of the garment is complete, leaving the rounded edge.

Invisible Casting Off

The complement to invisible casting on is a related method for casting off. Like the casting on this is suitable for use on K1, P1 rib and requires an odd number of loops.

It is begun on a right side row which begins with a knit stitch, when only about two rows more are required to be knitted to give the necessary depth.
Next row K1, *yarn forward, sl 1, yarn back, K1, rep from * to end.
Last row Yarn forward, sl 1, *yarn back, K1, yarn forward, sl 1, rep from * to end.
Break off the end leaving a length at least 3 times that of the edge being cast off and thread it into a wool needle.

Insert the needle into the first stitch as if to purl and draw the yarn through, insert it into the next st as if to knit and draw it through, leaving both stitches on the needle.

*Insert the needle into the first stitch again as if to knit, draw the yarn through and slip the stitch off the knitting needle. Take the needle in front of the next stitch

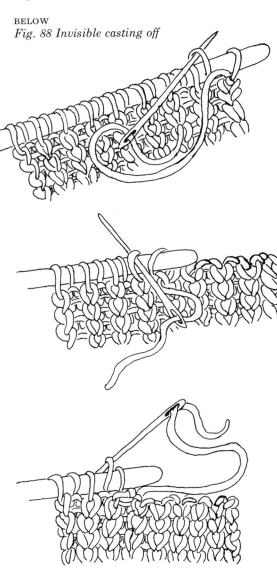

121

and insert it into the following stitch as if to purl and draw it through, leaving it on the knitting needle. Insert the needle into the first stitch on the knitting needle as if to purl, draw the yarn through and slip it off the knitting needle. Take the needle behind the next st into the back of the following stitch as if to knit and draw the yarn through, then take the yarn under the point of the knitting needle and repeat from * until all the stitches have been worked off.

Cords

A fine garment can be spoilt by laces which are uneven or skimpy, while a properly made cord makes all the difference. Cords can be knitted with only two or three stitches on double-pointed needles, returning the row always to the right end of the needle and never turning the needles round; they can also be plaited.

Finger knitting, however, makes an even better finish and can be worked in more than one colour and to any thickness required.

Finger Knitting

Two lengths of yarn are required and can be made of single or double thickness, self-coloured or mixed colours or can have one strand using two strands of one colour while the second strand uses two strands of another colour.

Knot the ends of both strands together and make a slip knot as for casting on, immediately above the knot.

Place the loop on the index finger of the right hand and hold the knot with the left thumb and finger. Take one length of yarn in the right hand and one in the left.

*Use the right index finger to draw a loop of yarn from the left strand through the original loop, making a new loop on the same finger. Draw the right strand gently until the loose yarn is removed and the newly made knot sits on top of the original knot. Bend the index finger under the strand in the right hand and draw the next loop through, drawing it into place by pulling gently on the left strand. Repeat from * until the cord begins to take shape. Once tried it can be worked quickly and makes an excellent trimming for all ties and can be used in bunches in place of untidy tassels.

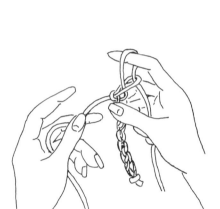

Fig. 89 Finger knitting cords

10 Northern Lace

PREVIOUS PAGE
120 Lace knitting in Unst. *National Museum of Antiquities of Scotland, Edinburgh*

It might be assumed that the finest lace knitting would be found in rich areas where the sophistication of court life and the money spent on trimmings of the latest fashion go hand in hand. But this is not so where knitted lace is concerned. It is to the most remote areas that attention must be turned, to Iceland, to Russia, to the Faroe Islands and to the most northerly of the islands of the Shetland group, Unst.

It is here in quiet homes, often far from the nearest neighbour, that gossamer fine wool is transformed into the cobweb-like beauty of shawl and stole, scarf and christening robe, where at one time even bridal veils were knitted.

ESSENTIALS FOR LACE

Two essential requirements are necessary before lace knitting can exist: firstly sheep with wool that is fine enough to be used for this purpose, and secondly spinners with the ability to draw out the wool into almost single-hair thickness.

In Unst, only the finest wool plucked, or rooed, by hand from the neck of the sheep was traditionally used for this lace yarn, and many a fine spinner of ordinary wool had no feeling for this work which was left to the few experts.

ORIGIN

The earliest mention of lace is found in the first part of the nineteenth century. However, the skill of the knitters must have existed before this and as early as 1790 stockings recorded as coming from Unst were being sold in Edinburgh at a higher price than the average woollen stocking.

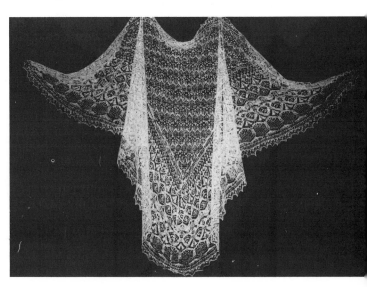

121 Cobweb perfection. *Lerwick Museum and Library, Shetland*

It seems most probable that samples of lace from Europe were shown to knitters who immediately saw the possibilities for their own craft. Sometimes attributed to the influence of Spain, the lace knitted in Unst certainly uses similar techniques to many Spanish laces, but this would seem inevitable in developing knitting in lace patterns. Methods for creating holes are few and any knitting that is to be used as a shawl, where right and wrong side are of almost equal importance, is likely to use garter stitch-based patterns that will remain flat and uncurling. It is hardly surprising that many stories revolve round the origin of this exquisite knitting and if ever there is a case for confusing fancy with fact it must surely be when attempting to discover the origins of this perfect lace.

Jessie Saxby, writing in a booklet published in Lerwick, recounts three legends, in which lace knitting is attributed to be an answer to prayer by a knitter seeking to benefit the land she loves, or as a skill given to a lame girl by a Troll or fairy who whispers to her to copy the web of the spider. But it is the third legend that perhaps captures the incredible lightness and delicacy of the lace, for it tells of a mermaid, who, unfitted for a land visit to the fisherman she loved, wove the sea foam into an elegant robe which so enchanted the islanders that they rushed to copy it as nearly as their resources allowed.

The records of Miss Saxby are not all fictitious, for not only does she attribute the start of lace knitting to 1832, which may well be reasonably accurate, but she also says that she has seen nothing finer than this lace, except for a shawl of Russian lace in an Edinburgh museum.

RUSSIAN LACE

Russian lace, as can be seen from the examples (*122, 123*), both in the collection at the Victoria and Albert Museum, London, is at the same time similar and dissimilar to the lace of Unst. The very fine centre stitch is certainly also seen in Unst knitting and in coarser knitting in other countries. The flower pattern is interesting and is only slightly different from the pine tree of Shetland. The largest motif on the border is quite unlike the Unst designs, although the treatment of the edge of the large diamond shapes is to be found on shell-shaped designs of Unst where the centres of the shells carry different filling stitches.

TECHNIQUE

The lightness and cobweb-like quality of Unst knitting is enhanced in every way. Wherever possible all firm edges, such as cast-on and cast-off edges, are eliminated, so that

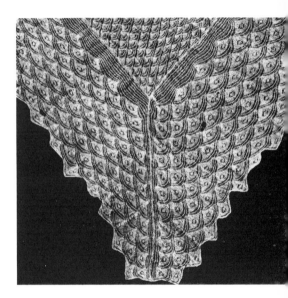

122 Russian lace with small patterns. *Victoria and Albert Museum, London*

a large shawl really can be drawn through a wedding ring – hence the name of ring shawls. A six-foot shawl may weigh less than two ounces but requires something in the region of three and a half miles of the finest wool to make.

Worked from the lace edge inwards, only grafting is used to join edges, again avoiding the harshness and bulk caused by seaming. A high degree of skill used to best advantage is seen in the completion of the shawls. Washed and possibly rinsed in a very small quantity of starch, the wet shawl is strung onto an adjustable frame. A lacing thread passed through the tip of each lace point of the finished shawl before washing is used to secure it to the numerous wooden pegs round the rim. On this frame the shawl is allowed to dry naturally before being removed and carefully folded away.

VARIATION ON A THEME

The islanders of Unst need no instructions, for their fingers and eyes together follow the pattern, using their knowledge of stitches to create a new design or to knit again an already successful one.

Much of the skill of lace knitting lies in combining simple patterns to make repeats which contrast openwork against solid areas, and areas of openwork against each other, each having a different degree of openness to add to whole.

This use of pattern can be seen clearly in the shawl shown here (*125*). Towards the inner edge of the border is a motif which is used in many different ways: as a tiny branched tree, a group of small trees filling a larger area, or a large tree standing alone on a solid background. Its shape makes it of great use because without vast calculations it can be altered in size just as the knitter requires.

It is, however, a small step from this to the Spider's Web which is almost like two trees worked from the base of one to its tip and then from the tip of the other back to the base, although the method of working makes the two sections not quite identical. The Spider's Web can be in its simplest form (*126*) or it can be adapted, increased in size and the central area between the two shapes filled with a tiny pattern to give one of the very beautiful panels in the centre of a shawl (*125*). The other panel which alternates with the Spider's Web lace completes this picture in every sense, for it is a related stitch, quite naturally called 'the spider'.

Special abbreviation

SK2togP   sl 1, K2 tog, psso.

Spider's Web Lace

Cast on a number of sts divisible by 10, plus 1.

1st row K3, *K2 tog, yon, K1, yon, K2 tog, K5, rep from *, ending last rep K3.

2nd row K2, *K2 tog, yon, K3, yon, K2 tog, K3, rep from *, ending last rep K2.

3rd row K1, *[K2 tog, yon] twice, K1, [yon, K2 tog] twice, K1, rep from * to end.

4th row [K2 tog, yon] twice, *K3, yon, K2 tog, yon, K3 tog, yon, K2 tog, yon, rep from * to last 7 sts, K3, [yon, K2 tog] twice.

5th row Work as for 3rd row.

6th row Work as for 2nd row.

7th row Work as for 1st row.

8th row K4, *yon, SK2togP, yon, K7, rep from *, ending last rep K4.

9th row K3, *yon, K2 tog, K1, K2 tog, yon, K5, rep from *, ending last rep K3.

10th row K2, *yon, K2 tog, yon, SK2togP, yon, K2 tog, yon, K3, rep from *, ending last rep K2.

11th row K1, *[yon, K2 tog] twice, K1, [K2 tog, yon] twice, K1, rep from * to end.

12th row Work as for 10th row.

13th row Work as for 9th row.

14th row Work as for 8th row.

These 14 rows form the pattern and can be repeated or used as a panel separated from another panel by 2 or more knit rows.

Spider Lace

In this version the spiders are placed alternately and the pattern repeats over 12 rows. The distance between the

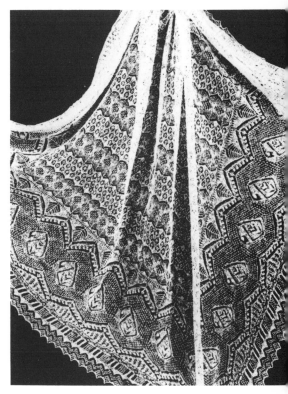

125 Unst lace shawl. *National Museum of Antiquities of Scotland, Edinburgh*

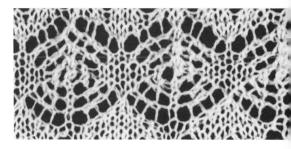

126 Spider's Web pattern

spiders can be altered and the number of rows worked between the lines of spiders can be increased to give a larger repeat.

Cast on a number of sts divisible by 8, plus 2.
1st row K1, *K2, K2 tog, yon, K1, yon, K2 tog, K1, rep from * to last st, K1.
2nd row K1, *K2 tog, yon, K3, yon, K2 tog, K1, rep from * to last st, K1.
3rd row K1, *K2, yon, K2 tog, yon, K3 tog, yon, K1, rep from * to last st, K1.
4th row K1, *K1, yon, K2 tog, K1, K2 tog, yon, K2, rep from * to last st, K1.
5th row K1, *K3, yon, SK2togP, yon, K2, rep from * to last st, K1.
6th row K1, *K2, yon, SK2togP, yon, K3, rep from * to last st, K1.
7th row K2, *yon, K2 tog, K3, K2 tog, yon, K1, rep from * to end.
8th row K1, *K1, yon, K2 tog, K1, K2 tog, yon, K2, rep from * to last st, K1.
9th row K1, *yon, K3 tog, yon, K3, yon, K2 tog, rep from * to last st, K1.
10th row K1, K2 tog, yon, *K3, yon, K2 tog, K1, K2 tog, yon, rep from * to last 7 sts, K3, yon, K2 tog, K2.
11th row K1, K2 tog, yon, *K5, yon, SK2togP, yon, rep from * to last 7 sts, K5, yon, K2 tog.
12th row K2 tog, yon, *K5, yon, SK2togP, yon, rep from * to last 8 sts, K5, yon, K2 tog, K1.
Rep 1st–12th rows as required.

That, however, is not the end of the theme. The complex curving lines and arrow-shaped solid areas in the tray cloth (*127*) may look unlike Spider's Web lace. A closer scrutiny shows just what making the most of known stitches can produce, for the two sections of Spider's Web lace have been used, worked on a half-drop principle where the second half has been worked not in its usual position but in the chevron shape lying between the first sections. Although this and the panel which leads on from it are in fact directional and therefore do not end with an exact repeat, the pattern is so balanced that this in no way detracts from the beauty of the finished cloth.

PATTERN PRESERVATION

Patterns can be hard to revive if they are intricate and knitters have forgotten how they were made. With an oral tradition like that on Unst some have feared that the variations might be forgotten, lost to those who follow.

It was for this reason that Mrs Elizabeth Henry, around the end of the nineteenth century, noted down patterns that she saw being worked in Shetland. That Mrs Henry

127 Tray cloth in fine thread. *Lerwick Museum and Library, Scotland*

had vision is without doubt, but she also had the energy to tackle the task and using a shorthand of her own wrote out pattern after pattern.

Born in Macduff, Mrs Henry had first hopes of becoming a surgeon but eventually had to be content with training at both Moray House in Edinburgh and at St Andrews University. It was at some time later than 1894, after she had been appointed Vice Principal of Sheffield Training College, that she spent time in Shetland and became involved in recording the patterns she saw being knitted. She stayed with the Sutherland family and wrote of how the father read his testament in Greek and Mrs Sutherland and her two daughters earned a living by their knitting; they had a natural culture – the womenfolk were members of the local orchestra in Lerwick, playing the violin and cello, and as they spun their wool they would sing old Norwegian songs.

In the following patterns which she recorded can be seen the simple effective use of the basic stitches, uncomplicated in their lack of complex increases or decreases, without stitches turned or twisted for effect and with none of the difficulties of patterns with rows continually changing their number of stitches.

Irish Lace Edging
Whether this was ever used in Ireland or whether it was named because of a likeness to the fine crochet made in Irish convents remains unknown, but it is both simple and effective as a lace for shawls or for household articles.

Cast on 20 sts.
1st row Sl 1, K1, [yon, K2 tog] 4 times, K3, K2 tog, yon, K3, yon, K2.
2nd row Yon, K2 tog, K19.
3rd row Sl 1, K2, [yon, K2 tog] 3 times, K3, K2 tog, yon, K5, yon, K2.
4th row Yon, K2 tog, K20.
5th row Sl 1, K1, [yon, K2 tog] 3 times, K3, K2 tog, yon, [K2 tog] twice, y3on, K2 tog, K1, yon, K2.
6th row Yon, K2 tog, K3, [K1 P1 K1] into loops of y3on, P1, K15.
7th row Sl 1, K2 [yon, K2 tog] 3 times, K4, yon, K2 tog, K3, K2 tog, yon, K2 tog, K1.
8th row Yon, K2 tog, K20.
9th row Sl 1, K1, [yon, K2 tog] 4 times, K4, yon, K2 tog, K1, K2 tog, yon, K2 tog, K1.
10th row Yon, K2 tog, K19.
11th row Sl 1, K2, [yon, K2 tog] 4 times, K4, yon, K3 tog, yon, K2 tog, K1.
12th row Yon, K2 tog, K18.
Rep 1st–12th rows as required.

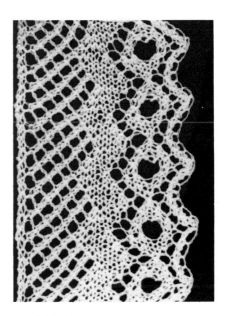

128 Irish lace edging

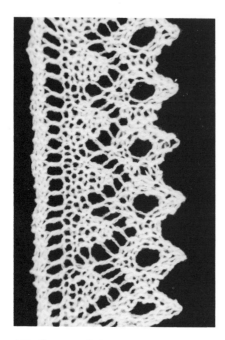

129 Cyprus edging

130 Wave pattern edging

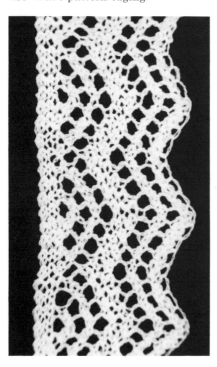

Cyprus Edging
Dainty and lost from stitch collections of recent years, this lace has many uses.

Cast on 12 sts.
1st row Sl 1, K5, K2 tog, yon, K1, K2 tog, K1.
2nd row K4, yon, K2 tog, K2, yon, K2 tog, K1.
3rd row Sl 1, K3, K2 tog, yon, K1, K2 tog, K2.
4th row K7, yon, K2 tog, K1.
5th row Sl 1, K4, yon, K2 tog, K1, y2on, K2.
6th row K2, [K1, P1] into 2 sts made by y2on on previous row, K2, yon, K3, yon, K2 tog, K1.
7th row Sl 1, K6, yon, K2 tog, K4.
8th row Cast off 2 sts, K2, yon, K5, yon, K2 tog, K1.
Rep 1st–8th rows as required.

Wave Pattern Edging
There are many different variations of wave patterned laces but this is easy to follow and makes a neat edging contrasting openwork against more solid areas to the best advantage.

Cast on 12 sts.
1st row Sl 1, K3, yon, K2 tog, K2, yon, K2 tog, yon, K2.
2nd and every alt row Yon, K2 tog, K to end.
3rd row Sl 1, K2, [yon, K2 tog] twice, K2, yon, K2 tog, yon, K2.
5th row Sl 1, K3, [yon, K2 tog] twice, K2, yon, K2 tog, yon, K2.
7th row Sl 1, K2, [yon, K2 tog] 3 times, K2, yon, K2 tog, yon, K2.
9th row Sl 1, K2, K2 tog, yon, K2 tog, yon, K2, K2 tog, [yon, K2 tog] twice, K1.
11th row Sl 1, K1, K2 tog, yon, K2 tog, yon, K2, K2 tog, [yon, K2 tog] twice, K1.
13th row Sl 1, K2, K2 tog, yon, K2, K2 tog, [yon, K2 tog] twice, K1.
15th row Sl 1, K1, K2 tog, yon, K2, K2 tog, [yon, K2 tog] twice, K1.
16th row Yon, K2 tog, K10.
Rep 1st–16th rows as required.

Coburg Lace Edging
Sharp points emphasized by parallel sloping lines make a lace that is smartly geometric.

Cast on 20 sts.
1st row Sl 1, K2, yon, K2 tog, K1, [yon, K2 tog] twice, K1, [yon, K2 tog] 3 times, y2on, K2 tog, K1.

2nd row K2, [K1, P1] in y2on from previous row, K11, yon, K2 tog, K4.

3rd row Sl 1, K2, yon, K2 tog, K1, [yon, K2 tog] twice, K2, [yon, K2 tog] 3 times, y2on, K2 tog, K1.

4th row K2, [K1, P1] in y2on of previous row, K12, yon, K2 tog, K4.

5th row Sl 1, K2, yon, K2 tog, K1, [yon, K2 tog] twice, K3, [yon, K2 tog] 3 times, y2on, K2 tog, K1.

6th row K2, [K1, P1] in y2on of previous row, K13, yon, K2 tog, K4.

7th row Sl 1, K2, yon, K2 tog, K1, [yon, K2 tog] twice, K4, [yon, K2 tog] 3 times, y2on, K2 tog, K1.

8th row K2, [K1, P1] in y2on of previous row, K14, yon, K2 tog, K4.

9th row Sl 1, K2, yon, K2 tog, K1, [yon, K2 tog] twice, K5, [yon, K2 tog] 3 times, y2on, K2 tog, K1.

10th row K2, [K1, P1] in y2on of previous row, K15, yon, K2 tog, K4.

11th row Sl 1, K2, yon, K2 tog, K1, [yon, K2 tog] twice, K6, [yon, K2 tog] 3 times, y2on, K2 tog, K1.

12th row K2, [K1, P1] in y2on of previous row, K16, yon, K2 tog, K4.

13th row Sl 1, K2, yon, K2 tog, K1, [yon, K2 tog] twice, K16.

14th row Cast off 6 sts, K13, yon, K2 tog, K4.

Rep 1st–14th rows as required.

Queen's Lace Edging

This lace is indeed fit for any queen. It has an unusual and most attractive straight edge and also a well pointed opposite edge which blocks ideally.

Cast on 12 sts.

1st row K4, yon, K2 tog, K2, yon, K2 tog, yon, K2.

2nd row K2, yon, K2 tog, yon, K5, yon, K2 tog, K2.

3rd row K1, K2 tog, yon, K7, yon, K2 tog, yon, K2.

4th row K2, yon, K2 tog, yon, K6, K2 tog, yon, K3.

5th row K4, yon, K2 tog, K3, K2 tog, yon, K1, yon, K2 tog, yon, K2.

6th row K2, yon, K2 tog, yon, K3, yon, K2 tog, K4, yon, K2 tog, K2.

7th row K1, K2 tog, yon, K4, K2 tog, yon, K5, yon, K2 tog, yon, K2.

8th row K2, yon, K2 tog, yon, K1, yon, K2 tog, K1, K2 tog, yon, K4, K2 tog, yon, K3.

9th row K4, yon, K2 tog, K4, yon, K3 tog, yon, K3, yon, K2 tog, yon, K2.

10th row K2, yon, K2 tog, yon, K5, yon, K2 tog, K6, yon, K2 tog, K2.

11th row K1, K2 tog, yon, K6, K2 tog, yon, K1, yon, K2

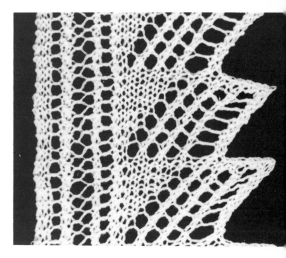

131 Coburg lace edging

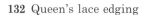

132 Queen's lace edging

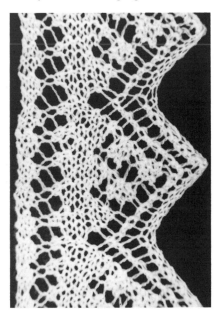

tog, K1, K2 tog, [yon, K2 tog] twice, K1.

12th row K1, K2 tog, yon, K2 tog, yon, K3 tog, yon, K3, yon, K2 tog, K3, K2 tog, yon, K3.

13th row K4, yon, K2 tog, K1, K2 tog, yon, K4, K2 tog, [yon, K2 tog] twice, K1.

14th row K1, K2 tog, [yon, K2 tog] twice, K1, K2 tog, yon, K5, yon, K2 tog, K2.

15th row K1, K2 tog, yon, K7, yon, K3 tog, [yon, K2 tog] twice, K1.

16th row K1, K2 tog, [yon, K2 tog] twice, K5, K2 tog, yon, K3.

17th row K4, yon, K2 tog, K3, K2 tog, [yon, K2 tog] twice, K1.

18th row K1, K2 tog, [yon, K2 tog] twice, K4, yon, K2 tog, K2.

19th row K1, K2 tog, yon, K4, K2 tog, [yon, K2 tog] twice, K1.

20th row K1, K2 tog, [yon, K2 tog] twice, K1, K2 tog, yon, K3.

Rep 1st–20th rows as required.

Print of the Wave Pattern

This pattern makes a lacy and very definite centre pattern and is used with very varied edges. There is also a shell pattern based on this which is unusual and most effective.

133 Print of the wave pattern. *Lerwick Museum and Library, Shetland*

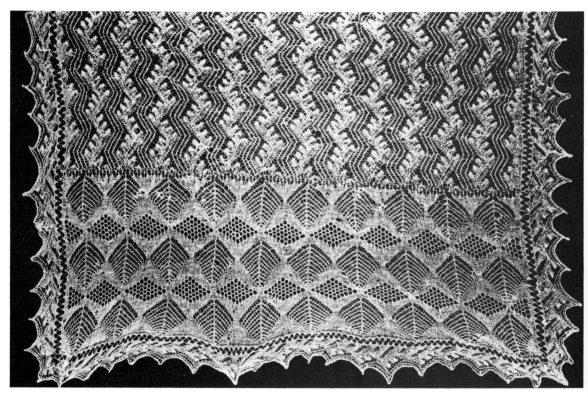

Special Abbreviation
SKP   sl 1, K1, psso.

Cast on a number of sts divisible by 24, plus 3.
1st row K4, *K2 tog, K3, [yon, K2 tog] 3 times, yon, K13,
rep from *, ending last rep K12.
2nd and every alt row P.
3rd row K3, *K2 tog, K3, yon, K1, yon [SKP, yon] 3 times,
K3, SKP, K7, rep from * to end.
5th row K2, *K2 tog, [K3, yon] twice, [SKP, yon] 3 times,
K3, SKP, K5, rep from * to last st, K1.
7th row K1, *K2 tog, K3, yon, K5, yon, [SKP, yon] 3 times,
K3, SKP, K3, rep from * to last 2 sts, K2.
9th row *K12, yon, [SKP, yon] 3 times, K3, SKP, K1, rep
from * to last 3 sts, K3.
11th row *K7, K2 tog, K3, [yon, K2 tog] 3 times, yon, K1,
yon, K3, SKP, rep from * to last 3 sts, K3.
13th row K6, *K2 tog, K3, [yon, K2 tog] 3 times, [yon, K3]
twice, SKP, K5, rep from *, ending last rep K2.
15th row K5, *K2 tog, K3, [yon, K2 tog] 3 times, yon, K5,
yon, K3, SKP, K3, rep from *, ending last rep, K1.
16th row P.
Rep 1st–16th rows as required.

Diamond and Fern Pattern
Another all-over pattern which shows the contrast
between openwork and more solid areas, so much part of
the beauty of this fine lace, combines lace diamonds with
the much used fern pattern.

Cast on a number of sts divisible by 16, plus 20.
1st row K2, K2 tog, yon, *K4, K2 tog, yon, K1, yon, K2
tog, K4, yon, SK2togP, yon, rep from * to last 16 sts, K4,
K2 tog, yon, K1, yon, K2 tog, K4, yon, K2 tog, K1.
2nd, 4th, 6th, 8th, 10th and 12th rows K.
3rd row K6, *K2 tog, yon, K1, yon, SK2togP, yon, K1, yon,
K2 tog, K7, rep from *, ending last rep K5.
5th row K4, *K2 tog, [yon, K1, yon, SK2togP] twice, yon,
K1, yon, K2 tog, K3, rep from * to end.
7th row K5, * [yon, SK2togP, yon, K1] twice, yon,
SK2togP, yon, K5, rep from *, ending last rep K4.
9th row K7, *yon, SK2togP, yon, K1, yon, SK2togP, yon,
K9, rep from *, ending last rep K6.
11th row K2, *yon, K2 tog, K5, yon, SK2togP, yon, K6, rep
from * to last 2 sts., yon, K2 tog.
13th row K2, K2 tog, yon, *K13, yon, SK2togP, yon, rep
from * to last 16 sts, K13, yon, K2 tog, K1.
14th row K2, K2 tog, yon, *K11, yon, K2 tog, K1, K2 tog,
yon, rep from * to last 16 sts, K11, yon, K2 tog, K3.
15th row K2, [K2 tog, yon] twice, *K9, yon, K2 tog, yon,

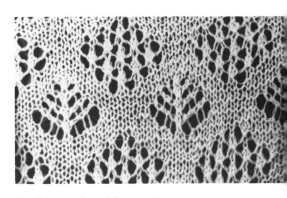

134 Diamond and fern pattern

SK2togP, yon, K2 tog, yon, rep from * to last 14 sts, K9, [yon, K2 tog] twice, K1.

16th row K2, [K2 tog, yon] twice, *K7, [yon, K2 tog] twice, K1, [K2 tog, yon] twice, rep from * to last 14 sts, K7, [yon, K2 tog] twice, K3.

17th row K2, [K2 tog, yon] twice, *K9, yon, K2 tog, yon, SK2togP, yon, K2 tog, yon, rep from * to last 14 sts, K9, [yon, K2 tog] twice, K1.

18th row K2, K2 tog, yon, *K11, yon, K2 tog, K1, K2 tog, yon, rep from * to last 16 sts, K11, yon, K2 tog, K3.

Rep 1st–18th rows as required.

Lace for a Shawl

Among the patterns recorded by Mrs Henry is this edging, named Alpine edging in modern collections. This version is more lacey and can be seen edging the tray cloth (*127*).

Cast on 24 sts.

1st row K5, yon, K2 tog, K5, yon, [K2 tog] twice, yon, K2 tog, K1, yon, K2 tog, yon, K3.

2nd row Yon, K2 tog, K1, yon, K2 tog, yon, K3, [K1, P1] both in next st, K2 tog, yon, K5, K2 tog, yon, K1, yon, K2 tog, K3.

3rd row K2, K2 tog, yon, K3, yon, K2 tog, K5, yon, [K2 tog] twice, yon, K2 tog, K1, yon, K2 tog, yon, K3.

4th row Yon, K2 tog, K1, yon, K2 tog, yon, K3, [K1, P1] both in next st, K2 tog, yon, K8, yon, K3 tog, yon, K4.

5th row K4, K2 tog, yon, K7, K2 tog, yon, K1, yon, [K2 tog] twice, yon, K2 tog, K1, yon, K2 tog, yon, K3.

6th row Yon, K2 tog, K1, yon, K2 tog, yon, K3, [K1 P1] both in next st, K2 tog, yon, K3, yon, K2 tog, K4, K2 tog, yon, K1, yon, K2 tog, K3.

7th row K2, K2 tog, yon, K3, yon, K2 tog, K2, K2 tog, yon, K5, yon, [K2 tog] twice, yon, K2 tog, K1, yon, K2 tog, yon, K3.

8th row Yon, [K2 tog] twice, [yon, K2 tog] twice, [K1, P1] both into next st, K3, yon, K2 tog, K1, K2 tog, yon, K6, yon, K3 tog, yon, K4.

9th row K4, K2 tog, yon, K8, yon, K3 tog, yon, K1, K2 tog, yon, [K2 tog] twice, [yon, K2 tog] twice, K2.

10th row Yon, [K2 tog] twice, [yon, K2 tog] twice, [K1, P1] both in next st, K3, yon, K2 tog, K6, K2 tog, yon, K1, yon, K2 tog, K3.

11th row K2, K2 tog, yon, K3, yon, K2 tog, K4, K2 tog, yon, K1, K2 tog, yon, [K2 tog] twice, [yon, K2 tog] twice, K2.

12th row Yon, [K2 tog] twice, [yon, K2 tog] twice, [K1, P1] both in next st, K3, yon, K2 tog, K5, yon, K3 tog, yon, K4.

13th row K5, K2 tog, yon, K4, K2 tog, yon, K1, K2 tog, yon, [K2 tog] twice, [yon, K2 tog] twice, K2.

Rep 2nd–13th rows as required.

11 Echoes from the Past

The slow change of a living tradition can suddenly be halted almost overnight by war or disaster, bringing to an end the settled way of life, dispersing the traditional crafts which may be destroyed forever or may appear, in an adapted form, in another country. Occasionally there is an echo from the past, strong enough to recall memories and possibly revive the traditions which have been so seriously curtailed.

ECHOES FROM ESTONIA

The Second World War radically changed the life of the islands off the Estonian coast, many of which became military zones after the invasion which ended Estonia's independence. But echoes of very expert knitting have come down the years, mainly due to the foresight of the Nordic Museum in Stockholm, founded in 1873. Here, recently, an exhibition reflected the life of a community hard put to make ends meet, but with an ability to knit to a very high standard of skill and design.

Picture island life, where fishing and hunting had to be added to the daily farming round to sustain the family. Homes were built from timber and wooden furniture, hand made utensils and pots, essentially for use, were devoid of colour. The tending of crops was mostly undertaken by the women, while men hunted seal with its added bonus of blubber as well as meat, or fished for eel or sprats. Festivals were few, the years of play for a child short, with work all summer and winter, in storm and in calm.

Against this softly toned background of wood, clay and straw, with unpainted walls and lack of decoration, knitting existed in shades of wool undreamed of unless seen. Vibrant flame vies with rich yellow for supremacy and the most brilliant of pinks, dimmed in no way by close proximity to the flame, is contrasted with dark violet, giving darkness without loss of colour. How this came into being may never be known, whether it was due to the inspiration of one knitter who, seeing the colours together, used them and started a trend, or whether the flower crop one summer inundated the island with marigolds or whatever was used to create these bold clear colours.

136 Stocking pattern from Mohn. *Nordic Museum, Stockholm*

Mohn

The island of Mohn, or Muhu in Estonian, used these colours more than the other islands of Runo (Ruhnu) or Ormso (Vormsi), where knitting was also of a very high standard.

Stockings from Mohn (*136*) have the legs worked in a banded pattern showing the use of flower shapes and delightful flying birds along with more geometric patterns,

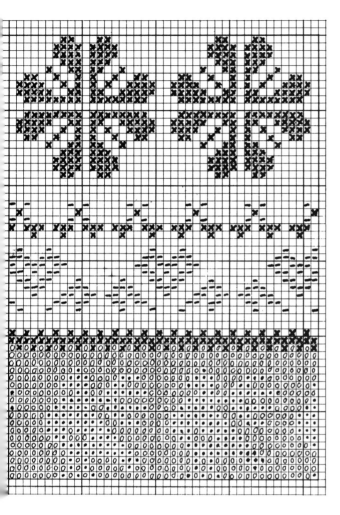

○ Pink
□ Flame
• White
× Violet
— Yellow

Fig. 90 Chart for Mohn stocking pattern (front cover design)

137 Gloves from Estonia. *Nordic Museum, Stockholm*

and the feet are worked in plain cream wool.

Gloves, using the same colours, are as interesting for their pattern as for the colouring. Small motifs, based on a square, are alternated, each the reverse of the one before.

In one chart (*fig. 91*) the motif is reversed in the use of the lines while in (*fig. 92*) the motifs are reversed in density, one being comparatively solid, the reverse open and light.

Runo

From Runo comes not only another form of patterning but also gloves in which, above a checked gauntlet edge, heavily fringed, there are bold line patterns worked in autumn greens and rust on a cream background. Above the main pattern on the back of the hand is placed a smaller, equally bold pattern and the plain fingers are each tipped with a tiny repeating pattern in green and

137

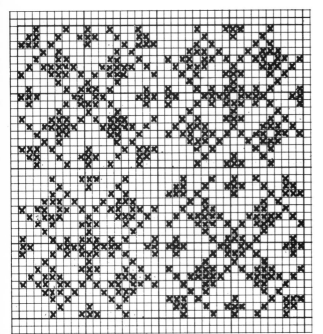

Fig. 91 Chart for glove pattern (1)

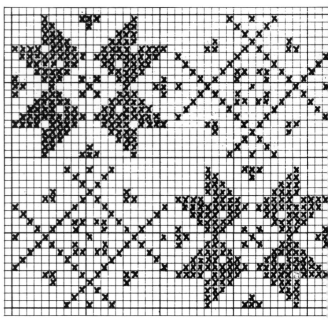

Fig. 92 Chart for glove pattern motifs (2)

Fig. 93 Chart for large glove pattern

□ Cream
• Green
× Dark green
○ Rust

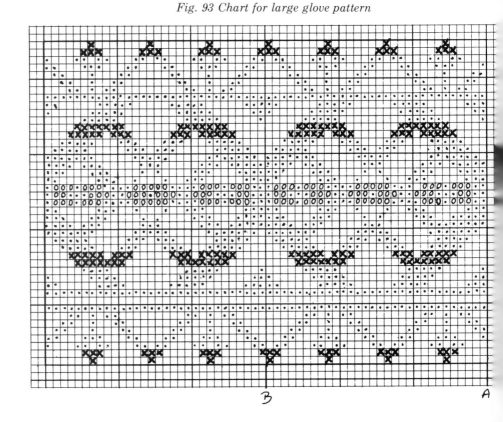

B   A

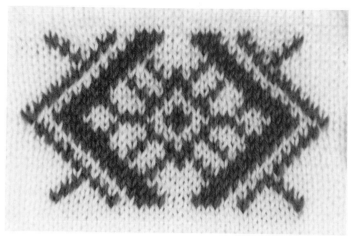

138 Large pattern from Runo gloves

139 Small pattern from Runo gloves

Fig. 94 Chart for small motif

rust as if they had been dipped into autumn (*139*).

Woven Knitting

The stockings on Runo (*140*) are quite different from the brilliantly coloured ones of Mohn and do not use stitches in contrasting patterns but yarns carried across the front of the work. The padded, almost embroidered, look makes the contrast greater and the pattern is clearer and more striking than if it had been knitted in.

To weave across the stitches marked in the charts (*figs. 96, 97*) the contrast yarn is brought to the front, the stitches it is to cover are then knitted in the background colour and the contrast yarn is carried across them and taken back, before the next background stitch is worked.

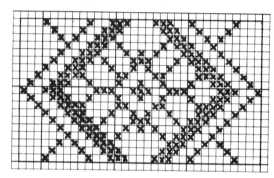

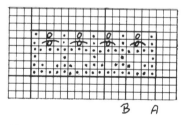

B   A

Fig. 95 Chart for finger tip pattern

140 Woven stockings from Runo.
Nordic Museum, Stockholm

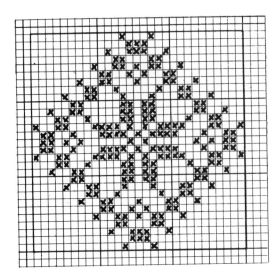

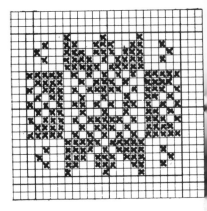

Fig. 97 Another woven pattern

Fig. 96 Chart for woven pattern

Knitted Lace

As on other northern islands, the wool could be spun into very fine yarn and lace shawls and stoles were knitted. Few examples remain, but the patterns are quite different from other laces. The stole in the last chapter (*158*) is an example using a most unusual bobble to contrast the solid cluster of threads against the fine open knitting. No yarn spun today gives quite the same effect as seen in the original, where the bobble seems intensely white against the surrounding strands.

Other Designs

Other less outstanding patterns come from the mainland and provide some borders or patterns which can be used equally for all-over patterns or as borders for a quicker result.

Flower and Chain Pattern

The flower is eight petalled (*141*), but the point used in Norway has been rounded off, and although not as shapely as the flower from Mohn, makes a design that is easily remembered and combines well with the vertical chain pattern. The chart (*fig. 98*) can also be reversed to give a horizontal variation where the flowers sit in borders above the linked chain.

Divided Diamond Pattern

This all-over pattern (*142*), with obvious border potential, is interesting in its link with the patterns of both Finland and Russia.

The Russian lace shawl (*123*) is worked in a lace stitch i a similar branching effect from the sides of the large diamond and a bolder version of this treatment is to be found in the two-coloured patterns of Finland.

141 Flower and chain pattern

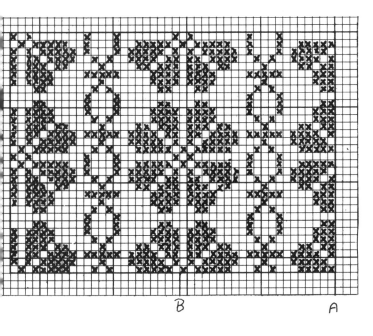

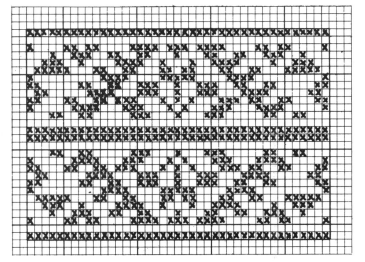

142 Divided diamond pattern

Fig. 98 Chart for flower and chain pattern

Fig. 99 Chart for divided diamond pattern

ECHOES FROM DENMARK

In the Museum of Falster Minders at Nykøbing, on the most southerly of the Danish islands, are to be found examples of stitch patterns unlike the patterns usually found on the Danish knitted blouse, worn under a top waistcoat and in use from about the end of the eighteenth century until the end of the nineteenth.

Danish Damask Pattern

The contrast of purl stitches against a plain stocking stitch background is the first method of varying knitting and of introducing pattern. Diagonal lines are amongst

141

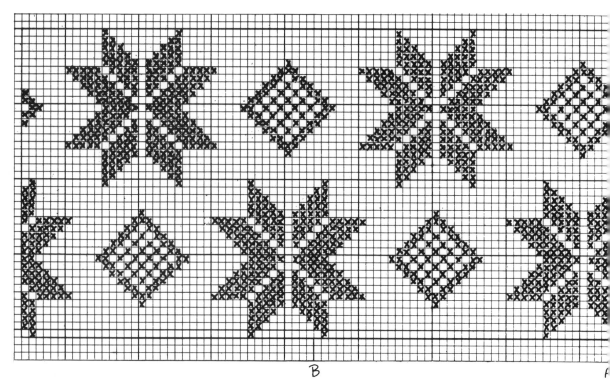

B   A

TOP
Fig. 100 Chart for Danish damask

ABOVE
143 Wearing Danish costume with a knitted blouse, at Aarhus

the simplest patterns to evolve, whether the knitters were originating patterns or trying to reproduce the woven fabrics around them.

In the simple top knitted in red, black or a dark greeny-blue fine wool, the knitters of Denmark produced designs very similar to those woven in damask. But in the Danish pattern there is one exception, for the eight sided star, although retaining its eight points, is worked in six sections, omitting the dividing lines on the side sections.

It is most easily worked from a diagram or chart where the smooth surface is left blank and the marks represent the purl stitches as seen from the right side of the work.

Falstar Style

The damask pattern is used on some of the examples in Falstar Minders Museum but seldom alone or without variations. Black and white photography does not do full justice to the clever placing and inter-relation between the stitches. Ribbon fold cabling may outline the edge of the shoulder and can be used on the sleeves which are always of importance and were the part of the garment which showed from under the waistcoat. Between the shoulders the same ribbon fold design is used, forming a deep yoke, but two wings or folds of it only turn away from each other with an area of purled stitches between, star-like, as if cast by the shadow of the ribbon.

Ribbon-fold Panel

The panel is worked over 11 sts.
Special abbreviations used are:

Tw2LB   sl next 2 sts knitwise to right needle then back to left needle in this position, pass right needle tip behind 1st st, Kb 2nd st but do not withdraw left needle, K 1st and 2nd sts tog tbl and withdraw left needle from both sts.

Tw2L   sl next 2 sts knitwise to right needle then back to left needle in this position, P2 tog tbl but do not withdraw left needle, K 1st st again and withdraw left needle.

Tw2B   pass needle behind 1st st, Pb 2nd st but do not withdraw left needle, K 1st st and withdraw left needle from both sts.

Tw2LK   pass right needle behind 1st st, P 2nd st tbl but do not withdraw left needle, K 1st and 2nd sts tog tbl and withdraw left needle from both sts.

Tw2R   pass needle in front of 1st st, K 2nd st but do not withdraw left needle, P tog 1st and 2nd sts and withdraw left needle from both sts.

Tw2   K2 tog but do not withdraw left needle, Kb 1st st and withdraw left needle from both sts.

Tw2RK   K2 tog but do not withdraw left needle, P 1st st and withdraw left needle

1st row P1, Tw2LB, P8.
2nd row K7, Tw2L, Pb1, K1.
3rd row P1, Kb1, P1, Tw2LB, P6.
4th row K5, Tw2L, [Pb1, K1] twice.
5th row P1, [Kb1, P1] twice, Tw2LB, P4.
6th row K3, Tw2L, [Pb1, K1] 3 times.
7th row P1, [Kb1, P1] 3 times, Tw2LB, P2.
8th row K1, Tw2L, [Pb1, K1] 4 times.
9th row P1, [Kb1, P1] 5 times.
10th row [K1, Pb1] 4 times, Tw2B, K1.
11th row P2, Tw2LK, [P1, Kb1] 3 times, P1.
12th row [K1, Pb1] 3 times, Tw2L, K3.
13th row P4, Tw2LK, [P1, Kb1] twice, P1.
14th row [K1, Pb1] twice, Tw2L, K5.
15th row P6, Tw2LK, P1, Kb1, P1.
16th row K1, Pb1, Tw2L, K7.
17th row P8, Tw2, P1.
18th row K1, Pb1, Tw2R, K7.
19th row P6, Tw2, P1, Kb1, P1.
20th row [K1, Pb1] twice, Tw2R, K5.
21st row P4, Tw2, P1, [Kb1, P1] twice.
22nd row [K1, Pb1] 3 times, Tw2R, K3.
23rd row P2, Tw2, P1, [Kb1, P1] 3 times.
24th row [K1, Pb1] 4 times, Tw2R, K1.
25th row P1, [Kb1, P1] 5 times.

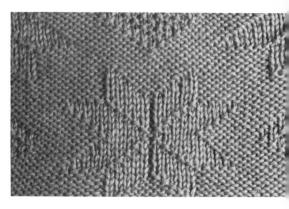

144 Danish damask pattern

145 Ribbon fold pattern

146 Damask pattern. Nordic
Museum, Stockholm

26th row K1, Tw2R, [Pb1, K1] 4 times.
27th row P1, [Kb1, P1] 3 times, Tw2RK, P2.
28th row K3, Tw2R, [Pb1, K1] 3 times.
29th row P1, [Kb1, P1] twice, Tw2RK, P4.
30th row K5, Tw2R, [Pb1, K1] twice.
31st row P1, Kb1, P1, Tw2RK, P6.
32nd row K7, Tw2R, Pb1, K1.
Rep 32 rows as required.

Many of the patterns used are large and suitable for a
one-size garment worked out originally to fit into an exact
space. The Swedish version of one star linked by
intercrossing moss stitch lines is typical of the large
design, but the usually square-shaped neck, shoulder area
and sleeve top edging were never left without their own
area of pattern which used a related moss stitch pattern
or a smaller travelling stitch design.

12 Patterns from East and West

147 Macedonian dancer wearing knitted stockings. *BBC Hulton Picture Library, London*

In Finland knitting takes second place to weaving but it still reflects an old tradition. As in many countries where knitting is not the leading handcraft, the shapes and colours used are similar to those of the traditional embroidery.

Two reasons contributed to knitting not existing in Finland before the eighteenth century: firstly, the comparative wealth of the Finns which allowed for the purchase of materials and meant less need for economy and secondly, the use of a form of single-needle knitting or coiling, as in Sweden. In fact until very recently, it was said that 'a man whose mittens were knitted had a poor wife'. The fabric made from the durable needle technique took pride of place and was an indication of a woman's skill.

148 Finnish border pattern

FINNISH PATTERNS
The variety of patterns on mittens, which are amongst the main knitted items, is great and shows both western and eastern influence.

Bold Cross Border
The fine lines and more subtle shapes of Shetland are forgotten in diagonal lines which are bold and decisive, forming a fretwork on the background (*148*).

These patterns are mostly worked in two boldly contrasting colours, but not always and if a third colour is introduced it is usually in a bold streak across the pattern, only two yarns being handled at any one time.

This pattern repeats over 24 stitches and is fascinating to knit.

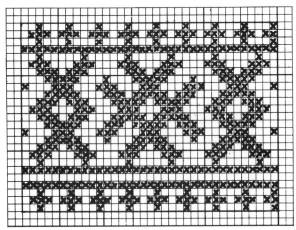

Fig. 101 Chart for Finnish border

RIGHT
Fig. 102 Chart for intricate border

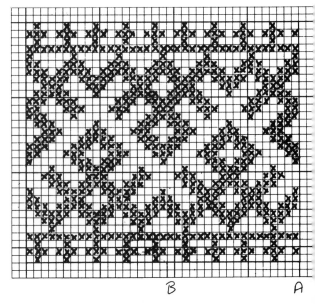

B   A

Fretwork Border

The differences between the previous pattern and this more complicated design are obvious but there is a subtlety which can only be appreciated as the stitches are worked. The construction is so simple for the knitter that it is almost bewildering. In coloured patterns the row being worked always determines the row to come, because nearly all patterns build up their lines only to reduce them again, but the clarity of this is never so obvious as in these Finnish patterns.

Most dramatic in one contrasting colour, it can have the pattern divided into three sections, the outer two being worked in one contrast, possibly black on white or cream and the centre rows worked in red on cream or white.

All-over Pattern

The chart (*fig. 103*) shows the changes that are needed to make the first border pattern into an all-over pattern.

This pattern, like the others, with its comparatively even distribution of pattern and background will give surprising results in different colours. With some colours the fretwork is formed by the shapes that look like the pattern and with others the fretwork will seem to be the background shapes which have moved into prominence.

Seeding

In many mitten patterns, and larger garments, seeding is used between main patterns, much as it is used in Norway.

Looped Knitting

Looped knitting is often used to decorate the edge of gauntlets, making a fringe that wears considerably better than a cut fringe which in some yarns becomes bedraggled with friction.

149 Intricate border pattern

Fig. 103 Chart for alteration to all-over pattern

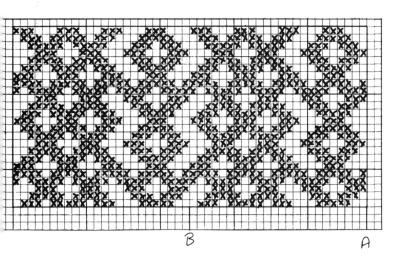

Looped knitting can be worked in two ways, either

1 Round the fingers
2 Round a card or ruler

In each method the loop is formed on a wrong-side row and the method of winding the strands round a ruler produces the most even fringe.

Finger Method

On a wrong-side row knit the first stitch. Insert the needle into the next stitch, hold one or even two fingers behind the needle tip which is through the stitch and wrap the yarn twice or three times round the fingers and right needle tip before drawing the loops through. To complete the stitch, slip the loops back to the left needle and knit them together.

Ruler Method

This is worked similarly but requires two rows to complete the knitting in of the loops.

On a wrong-side row hold a ruler or strip of card of the depth of fringe required behind the right-hand needle. As each stitch is knitted, using double or triple strands of yarn, take the yarn round the card before drawing all the strands through the stitch. Repeat this in every stitch to the end of the row.

On the second row use only the yarn that the garment is being made of and knit together the stitch and the double or triple strands that were drawn through each stitch.

Both methods can be used for a single row of fringe or can be repeated on alternate rows (wrong-side rows) until the fringe is the depth required.

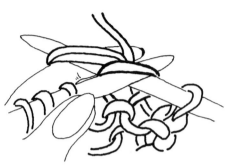

Fig. 104 Knitting in loops made round the finger

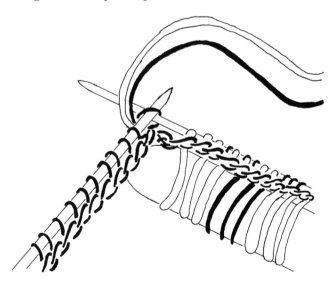

Fig. 105 Knitting loops wound round a ruler

TURKISH KNITTING

The knitting of Turkey shows a strong traditional influence, not only from embroidery but also from Turkish skills in rug making. Knitting can be classified in districts by its similarity to the rug patterns used in the same area.

Although a twisted stitch was probably used at one time the socks which brighten the markets today are worked with untwisted stitches in shades of blues and red, touched with cream.

These three charts (*figs. 106–108*) each carry a wealth of patterns for coloured knitting which could be divided further or placed together to build up a very ornate panel just as is found in the socks, which are patterned from top to toe.

Turkey has also served as a meeting place for knitters of many countries as described by Miss Lambert, author of an early knitting book in 1844, writing of a visit made to a Fez factory by a Miss Pardoe:

As we passed the threshold a most curious scene presented itself. About five hundred females were collected together in a vast hall, awaiting the delivery of the wool which they were to knit and a more extraordinary group could not perhaps be found in the world. There was a Turkess with her yashmak folded closely over her face, and her dark feridjhe falling to the pavement; the Greek woman with her large turban and braided hair, covered loosely with a scarf of white muslin, her gay coloured dress and large shawl; the Armenian, with her dark eyes flashing from under the jealous screen of her carefully arranged veil, and her red slippers peeping out under the long wrapping cloak; the Jewess, muffled in a coarse linen cloth, and standing a little apart, as though she feared to offend by more immediate contact: and among the crowd some of the loveliest girls imaginable.

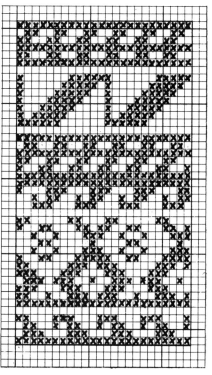

Fig. 107 Chart for second Turkish pattern

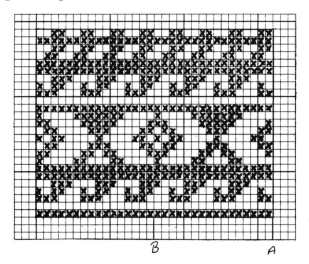

Fig. 106 Chart for first Turkish pattern

149

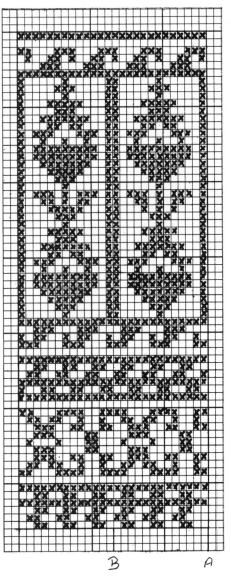

Fig. 108 Chart for third Turkish
pattern

B   A

YUGOSLAVIAN KNITTING

In Yugoslavia the stockings knitted in brilliant colours
are still part of the folk costume, knitted in the same
shape as they have been for centuries with a pointed toe
and an almost equally pointed heel. The socks from
Albania (*150*) show a technique which appears to be a
cross between knitting and crochet and may be worked
with a single needle.

The socks from all the surrounding territories look at
first glance as if they had been knitted onto already
woven or embroidered sections. It seems unlikely that two
different techniques should be used on one item so
domestic and everyday, so it may be time to look at which
technique is used.

In museums throughout Europe examples can be found
all labelled 'knitting', but a closer look at the wrong side
shows neat rows of chain loops only achieved with a
needle or even more likely, with a hook. They are worked
from the toe upwards, and, if not worked with a single
needle, might they not have been made on a series of
hooked needles as in Tunisian crochet? This is not so
unusual as might be expected, for fine wire hooked
needles have been found in an unfinished sock in Egypt
many hundreds of years old.

GREEK KNITTING

As in Turkey, knitting in Greece shows bold patterns but
uses even larger designs with only one repeat showing on
leg coverings such as these from Lamia. The yarn is harsh
and unyielding but exceedingly hardwearing, and is
knitted round. The patterns are used not only for footless

150 Albanian socks. *Victoria and
Albert Museum, London*

150

151 Greek leggings.
Kunstindustrimvseet, Copenhagen

stockings or gaiters but also for lower arm bands worn
below the full blouse which puffs out above the strong
pattern. Market stalls sell traditional knitting, seamless
and perfect, cut down the joining line, for making into
bags with two sections sewn together on the wrong side.

SOUTH AMERICAN KNITTING

Knitting came to South America from Spain and was
unknown in pre-conquest times, despite the fact that
textiles of great skill and immense decorative value had
been made from a very early date, long before Spanish
influence.

As in Europe, both examples of sprang and single-
needle knitting have been found and some examples of
work thought to be knitting have probably been made in
this way.

As so often, it is in the mountains and the rural areas
far from contact with other influences that the best of
knitting is to be found. In the foothills of the Andes
intricately shaped caps are knitted, often brilliantly
decorated with bright pinks and vivid rainbow colours. In
Peru and Bolivia patterns may seem familiar one moment
and then completely different, even on the same garment.

Technique

In Bolivia attention to the finishing touches creates ideas
not seen elsewhere and techniques which should have a
place in the expertise of all knitters.

Earflap shaping is interesting, because the flap is cast
on in the centre and worked outwards, including the
necessary shaping, and is folded in half after completion
before being attached to the sides of the cap.

This technique makes the outside edge the finished edge
but it has its own decoration for it is cast off with picot
knots giving it a knitted-in finish that adds a touch of
style.

The knots are worked wherever required and can be

spaced widely apart or packed closely together giving an almost frilled appearance.

Picot Cast Off

*Insert the needle through the first stitch and make a knot by casting on two stitches, knit them and cast both off again, then knit the next stitch. There are two stitches on the needle, cast off one by lifting it over the second in the usual way. The edge may be repeated from the * or more sts can be cast off before repeating if the knots or picots are to be spaced out.

Size of knot

The distance between the knots is controlled by the number of stitches cast off but the size of the knot can also be altered by casting on more than two stitches and casting them off again after knitting them, before the stitches between the knots are worked.

A frilled effect is given by working knots closely together.

PATTERNS

The charts (*figs. 109–111*) show three small patterns that may serve as an introduction to the very large subject of Peruvian and Bolivian patterns.

These are suitable for working with the stranding method but each pattern requires to be judged on its own, changing to using small bobbins and twisting the yarns at colour changes (see Argyll patterns, page 55) if the space between two uses of one colour is too great or where a great many colours are used for small areas.

The need for this constant assessment arises from the influence of weaving and embroidery and the continued use of traditional patterns that can be knitted but were not originally designed for knitting.

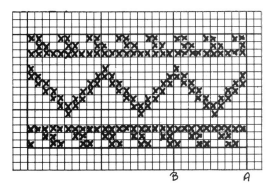

Fig. 109 Chart for Bolivian pattern

Fig. 110 Chart for Bolivian cat

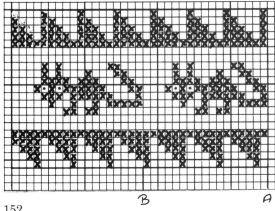

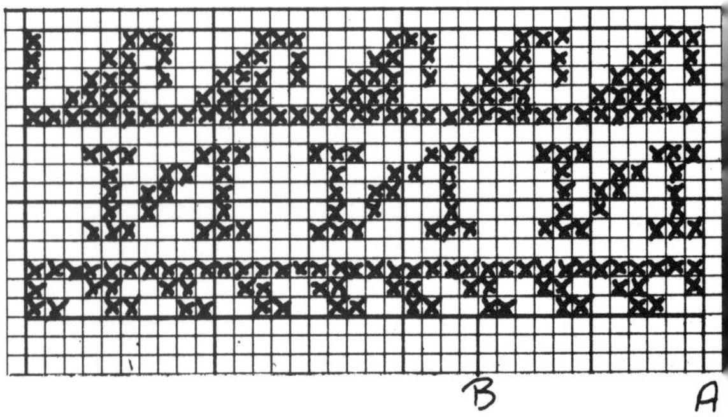

Fig. 111 Chart for another pattern from Bolivia

13 Traditional Patterns

PREVIOUS PAGE
152 Austrian waistcoat
(See page 158 for instructions)

Traditional patterns are always best when knitted in the way and in the yarn that would have been used by the knitters who worked the original designs.

The following patterns have been designed to give the opportunity to try out some of these traditional stitch patterns and knitting techniques.

SWEATER FROM ARAN

Although less complicated than many of the best examples of Aran knitting, this design is based on stitches which are in use and which make the most of the light and shade which the patterns form on the creamy, natural wool. It also retains the set-in sleeves which were used before commercialization stamped the use of raglan sleeves on every Aran garment. The ribbed welt is also part of the complete pattern, blending into the more intricate main pattern when the edging is complete. (See colour plate 3.)

Materials
15(16:17:18) 50 g balls of Templeton's Aran Wool
1 pair each 4 mm and 4½ mm needles
1 cable needle

Measurements
To fit a 85(90:95:100) cm bust/chest.
Length to shoulder: 61(63:65:67) cm or as required.
Sleeve seam: 45(45:46:47) cm or as required.

Tension
Equivalent to 18 sts and 24 rows to 10 cm on 4½ mm needles measured over st st.

Special Abbreviations

C3	sl next 2 sts to CN, hold at back, K next st, sl P st from CN to left needle and P it, K rem st from CN.
C6R	sl next 3 sts to CN, hold at back, K3, K3 from CN.
C6L	sl next 3 sts to CN, hold at front, K3, K3 from CN.
Tw2	pass right needle in front of 1st st on left needle, K 2nd st but do not withdraw the left needle, K the 1st st and withdraw the left needle from both sts.
Tw2L	pass right needle behind 1st st on left needle and K 2nd st tbl but do not withdraw left needle, K 1st st and withdraw the left needle from both sts.
RT	Pass in front of 1st st, K into front of 2nd st on left needle then P into 1st st withdrawing the left needle from both sts.
LT	Pass behind 1st st, P into 2nd st on left needle then K into 1st st withdrawing left needle from both sts.
MB	make a bobble by working [K1, yon, K1, yon, K1] all into next st, turn, P5, turn, K5, turn, P5, turn, sl 2, K3 tog, psso to complete bobble.

153 Detail of centre of Aran sweater

Panel A
Worked over 13 sts.
1st row K6, P1, K6.
2nd row P6, K1, P6.
3rd row K6, P1, K6.
4th row P6, K1, P6.
5th row C6R, P1, C6L.
6th row P6, K1, P6.
7th row K6, P1, K6.
8th row P6, K1, P6.
9th row K6, P1, K6.
10th row P6, K1, P6.
11th row C6L, P1, C6R.
12th row P6, K1, P6.
Rep 1st–12th rows throughout.

Panel B
Worked over 17 sts.
1st row P1, K1, [RT] 3 times, K1, [LT] 3 times, K1, P1.
2nd row K1, P15, K1.
3rd row P1, LT, [RT] twice, K3, [LT] twice, RT, P1.
4th row K2, P13, K2.
5th row P2, LT, [RT] twice, K1, [LT] twice, RT, P2.
6th row K3, P11, K3.
7th row P3, LT, RT, K3, LT, RT, P3.
8th row K4, P9, K4.
9th row P4, LT, RT, K1, LT, RT, P4.
10th row K5, P7, K5.
11th row P5, LT, K3, RT, K5.
12th row K6, P5, K6.
13th row P2, MB, P3, LT, K1, RT, P3, MB, P2.
14th row K7, P3, K7.
15th row P6, RT, K1, LT, P6.
16th row Work as for 12th row.
17th row P5, RT, K3, LT, P5.
18th row Work as for 10th row.
19th row P4, [RT] twice, K1, [LT] twice, P4.
20th row Work as for 8th row.
21st row P3, [RT] twice, K3, [LT] twice, P3.
22nd row Work as for 6th row.
23rd row P2, [RT] 3 times, K1, [LT] 3 times, P2.
24th row Work as for 4th row.
25th row P1, [RT] 3 times, K3, [LT] 3 times, P1.
26th row Work as for 2nd row.
Rep 1st–26th rows throughout.

Back
Using 4 mm needles cast on 86(93:100:107) sts.
1st row K2, *P1, K1, P1, K1, P1, K2, rep from * to end.
2nd row P2, *K1, P1, K1, P1, K1, P2, rep from * to end.
3rd row Work as for 1st row.
4th row Work as for 2nd row.

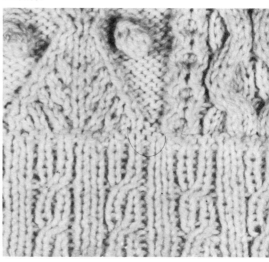

154 Detail of lower edge of Aran sweater

155

5th row K2, *P1, C3, P1, K2, rep from * to end.
6th row Work as for 2nd row.
Rep 1st–6th rows until welt measures 7 cm, ending with a wrong-side row.
Change to 4½ mm needles.
P1 row.
Increase row P, inc 15(14:13:12) times evenly across row. 101(107:113:119) sts.

Begin Pattern

1st row K17(19:21:23), P1, Tw2, Tw2L, P1, work panel A over next 13 sts, P1, Tw2, Tw2L, P1(2:3:4), work panel B over next 17 sts, P1(2:3:4), Tw2, Tw2L, P1, work panel A over next 13 sts, P1, Tw2, Tw2L, P1, K17(19:21:23).
2nd row K all K sts and P all P sts.
3rd row K17(19:21:23), P1, Tw2L, Tw2, P1, work panel A, P1, Tw2L, Tw2, P1(2:3:4), work panel B, P1(2:3:4), Tw2L, Tw2, P1, work panel A, P1, Tw2L, Tw2, P1, K17(19:21:23).
4th row K17(19:21:23), P all P sts and K all K sts to last 17(19:21:23) sts, K to end.
Rep last 4 rows throughout, rep panels A and B as required.
Work until 42(43:44:45) cm or required length to underarm, ending with a wrong-side row.

Shape Armholes

Cast off 4 sts at beg of next 2 rows.
Dec 1 st at each end of next and every foll alt row until 81(85:89:93) sts rem.
Work without shaping until armhole measures 19(20:21:22) cm, ending with a wrong side row.

Shape Shoulders

Cast off 5 sts at beg of next 8 rows.
Cast off 3(4:5:6) sts at beg of next 2 rows.
Leave rem 35(37:39:41) sts on holder for neckband.

Front

Work as for back until armholes measure 8 cm less to shoulder, ending with a wrong-side row.

Shape Neck

1st row Patt 32(33:34:35), turn. Leave rem sts on holder.
**Keeping patt correct dec 1 st at neck edge on next 5 rows then on right side rows only until 23(24:25:26) sts rem.
Work without shaping until same length as back to shoulder, ending at armhole edge.

Shape Shoulder

Cast off 5 sts at beg of next 4 alt rows.
Work 1 row.
Cast off rem sts**.
With right side facing slip centre 17(19:21:23) sts to holder.
Rejoin yarn to rem sts and work to end of row.
Complete as for other shoulder working from ** to **.

Sleeves

Using 4 mm needles cast on 37(37:44:44) sts.

Work welt as for back.

Change to 4½ mm needles.

P 1 row.

Increase row P, inc 8(10:5:7) sts evenly across row.
45(47:49:51) sts.

Begin Pattern

1st row K10(11:12:13), P1, Tw2, Tw2L, P1, work panel A
over next 13 sts, P1, Tw2, Tw2L, P1, K10(11:12:13).

2nd row K all K sts and P all P sts.

3rd row K10(11:12:13), P1, Tw2L, Tw2, P1, work panel A,
P1, Tw2L, Tw2, P1, K10(11:12:13).

4th row K10(11:12:13), P all P sts and K all K sts to last
10(11:12:13) sts, K to end.

Cont keeping patt correct and inc 1 st at each end of next
and every foll 8th row until there are 65(67:69:71) sts, rep
panel A as required, working increased sts into side
pattern.

Work until sleeve measures 45(45:46:47) cm or required
seam length, ending with a wrong-side row.

Shape Top

Cast off 4 sts at beg of next 2 rows.

Dec 1 st at each end of next 4 rows, then at each end of
every right side row until 21 sts rem.

Cast off 2 sts at beg of next 6 rows.

Cast off rem sts.

Work 2nd sleeve in the same way.

Neckband

Join right shoulder seam.

Using 4 mm needles and with right side of work facing K
up 16(17:16:17) sts down side of front neck, K across
17(19:21:23) sts from centre front, K up 16(17:16:17) sts
from other side of neck and K across 35(37:39:41) sts from
back inc 1 st in centre for 2nd size only and dec 1 st in
centre for 3rd size only.

84(91:91:98) sts.

K 1 row.

Begin Rib

1st row *K2, P1, [K1, P1] twice, rep from * to end.

2nd row *K1, [P1, K1] twice, P2, rep from * to end.

3rd and 4th rows Work as for 1st and 2nd rows.

5th row *K2, P1, C3, P1, rep from * to end.

6th row Work as for 2nd row.

Rep 1st and 2nd rows 6 times more.

Cast off in rib.

To Complete

Join left shoulder seam and neckband. Fold neckband in
half to wrong side and slip st in place.

155 Detail of sleeve pattern

Join side seams.
Seam sleeves and sew into armhole.

WAISTCOAT FROM AUSTRIA

Two distinct patterns are used for this waistcoat (*152*). A narrow panel of interwoven cable stitches outlines the front edges and is repeated on either side of a narrow central panel on the back. To either side of the panels is worked an all-over pattern which contrasts with the vertical lines of the cable pattern.

Many stitch patterns are seldom used in commercial patterns because the instructions cannot easily be condensed for the number of sizes that are given or so that the pattern is positioned correctly facing one way on the left side and the reverse way on the right side.

In the following instructions this is overcome by giving the patterns separately. The cable panel is given as panel C and worked over 14 stitches. It is used for both right and left front and at either side of the centre back panel.

The main all-over pattern is given for the left front and right back as panel A and for the right front and left back as panel B, both of which are worked over 36(40:44:48) stitches, depending on the size you are knitting.

The centre back panel is worked over six stitches and is panel D.

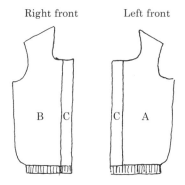

Fig. 112 Layout of panels for waistcoat

Right front   Left front

B C   C A

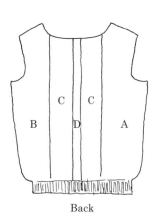

C C

B D A

Back

Materials

9(9:10:11) 25 g balls of Templeton's Ayrmist Double Knitting
1 pair each 3 mm and 3¾ mm needles
6 buttons

Measurements

To fit an 85(90:95:100) cm bust
Length to shoulder: 43(44:47:48) cm, or as required.

Tension

Equivalent to 12 sts and 16 rows to 5 cm measured over st st worked on 3¾ mm needles.

Special Abbreviations

C2BP   sl next st to CN, hold at back, K1, Pb1 from CN.
C2FP   sl next st to CN, hold at front, Pb1, K1 from CN.
Tw2F   K next 2 sts tog but do not withdraw left needle, K 1st st again and withdraw left needle.
Tw2B   pass right needle behind 1st st on left needle, K 2nd st tbl but do not withdraw left needle, K both sts tog tbl and withdraw left needle.

Main Panel A

Worked over 36(40:44:48) sts.
1st row For 1st and 3rd sizes only P4, for all sizes [P3, K1, P4] 4(5:5:6) times.

2nd row [K4, P1, K3] 4(5:5:6) times, working last 4(0:4:0) sts K4.

3rd row For 1st and 3rd sizes only K1, P3, for all sizes [P2, K1, P1, K1, P3] 4(5:5:6) times.

4th row [K3, P1, K1, P1, K2] 4(5:5:6) times, working last 4(0:4:0) sts K3, P1.

5th row For 1st and 3rd sizes only P1, K1, P2 for all sizes [P1, K1, P1, K1, P1, K1, P2] 4(5:5:6) times.

6th row [K2, P1, K1, P1, K1, P1, K1] 4(5:5:6) times, working last 4(0:4:0) sts K2, P1, K1.

7th and 8th rows Work as for 3rd and 4th rows.

9th and 10th rows Work as for 1st and 2nd rows.

11th row For 1st and 3rd sizes only P3, K1, for all sizes [P7, K1] 3(4:4:5) times, P8.

12th row K8, [P1, K7] 3(4:4:5) times, working last 4(0:4:0) sts P1, K3.

13th row For 1st and 3rd sizes only P2, K1, P1, for all sizes [K1, P5, K1, P1] 3(4:4:5) times, K1, P7.

14th row K7, P1, [K1, P1, K5, P1] 3(4:4:5) times, working last 4(0:4:0) sts K1, P1, K2.

15th row For 1st and 3rd sizes only [P1, K1] twice, for all sizes [P1, K1, P3, K1, P1, K1] 3(4:4:5) times, P1, K1, P6.

16th row K6, P1, K1 [P1, K1, P1, K3, P1, K1] 3(4:4:5) times, working last 4(0:4:0) sts [P1, K1] twice.

17th and 18th rows Work as for 13th and 14th rows.

19th and 20th rows Work as for 11th and 12th rows.

These 20 rows are repeated throughout left front and for right side of back.

Main Panel B

Worked over 36(40:44:48) sts.

1st row [P4, K1, P3] 4(5:5:6) times, working last 4(0:4:0) sts P4.

2nd row For 1st and 3rd sizes only K4, for all sizes [K3, P1, K4] 4(5:5:6) times.

3rd row [P3, K1, P1, K1, P2] 4(5:5:6) times, working last 4(0:4:0) sts P3, K1.

4th row For 1st and 3rd sizes only P1, K3, for all sizes [K2, P1, K1, P1, K3] 4(5:5:6) times.

5th row [P2, K1, P1, K1, P1, K1, P1] 4(5:5:6) times, working last 4(0:4:0) sts P2, K1, P1.

6th row For 1st and 3rd sizes only K1, P1, K2, for all sizes [K1, P1, K1, P1, K1, P1, K2] 4(5:5:6) times.

7th and 8th rows Work as for 3rd and 4th rows.

9th and 10th rows Work as for 1st and 2nd rows.

11th row P8, [K1, P7] 3(4:4:5) times, working last 4(0:4:0) sts K1, P3.

12th row For 1st and 3rd sizes only K3, P1, for all sizes [K7, P1] 3(4:4:5) times, K8.

13th row P7, K1, [P1, K1, P5, K1] 3(4:4:5) times, working last 4(0:4:0) sts P1, K1, P2.

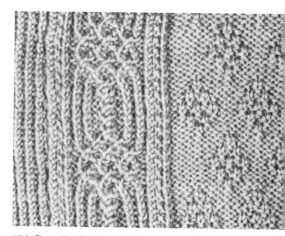

156 Detail of side and front panel of Austrian waistcoat

14th row For 1st and 3rd sizes only K2, P1, K1, for all sizes [P1, K5, P1, K1] 3(4:4:5) times, P1, K7.

15th row P6, K1, P1, [K1, P1, K1, P3, K1, P1] 3(4:4:5) times, working last 4(0:4:0) sts [K1, P1] twice.

16th row For 1st and 3rd sizes only [K1, P1] twice, for all sizes [K1, P1, K3, P1, K1, P1] 3(4:4:5) times, K1, P1, K6.

17th and 18th rows Work as for 13th and 14th rows.

19th and 20th rows Work as for 11th and 12th rows.

Repeat these 20 rows for right front and left side of back.

Cable Panel C

Worked over 14 sts.

1st row [P1, Kb1] twice, P2, Tw2F, P2, [Kb1, P1] twice.

2nd row [K1, Pb1] twice, K2, Pb2, K2, [Pb1, K1] twice.

3rd–9th rows Rep 1st and 2nd rows 3 times more then 1st row once.

10th row K1, Pb1, K1, [C2BP, C2FP] twice, K1, Pb1, K1.

11th row P1, Kb1, P2, [Tw2B, P2] twice, Kb1, P1.

12th row K1, [C2BP, C2FP] 3 times, K1.

13th row P2, [Tw2F, P2] 3 times.

14th row K1, [C2FP, C2BP] 3 times, K1.

15th row P1, Kb1, P2, [Tw2B, P2] twice, Kb1, P1.

16th row K1, [C2BP, C2FP] 3 times, K1.

17th row P2, [Tw2F, P2] 3 times.

18th row K1, [C2FP, C2BP] 3 times, K1.

19th row P1, Kb1, P2, [Tw2B, P2] twice, Kb1, P1.

20th row K1, Pb1, K1, [C2FP, C2BP] twice, K1, Pb1, K1.

These 20 rows are repeated throughout both front and back panels.

Centre Back Panel D

Worked over 6 sts.

1st row P1, Tw2F, P2, Kb1.

2nd row Pb1, K2, Pb2, K1.

3rd row Work as for 1st row.

4th row C2BP, C2FP, C2BP.

5th row Kb1, P2, Tw2B, P1.

6th row K1, Pb2, K2, Pb1.

7th row Work as for 5th row.

8th row C2FP, C2BP, C2FP.

Repeat these 8 rows throughout the length of the centre back panel.

157 Detail of centre back panel

Back

Using 3 mm needles cast on 111(119:127:135) sts.

1st row Kb1, *P1, Kb1, rep from * to end.

2nd row Pb1, *K1, Pb1, rep from * to end.

Rep 1st and 2nd rows 8 times more, then 1st row once.

Increase row Rib 2(6:10:14), M1, [rib 10, M1] 3 times, rib 9, M1, rib 14, K2 tog, rib 13, M1, rib 9, [M1, rib 10] 3 times, M1, rib 2(6:10:14). 120(128:136:144) sts.

Change to $3\frac{3}{4}$ mm needles and main pattern.

1st row Work panel A over next 36(40:44:48) sts, Kb1, P1, Kb1, work panel C over next 14 sts, [Kb1, P1] twice, work panel D for centre back over next 6 sts, [P1, Kb1] twice, work panel C over next 14 sts, Kb1, P1, Kb1, work panel B over last 36(40:44:48) sts.

2nd row Work panel B over next 36(40:44:48) sts, Pb1, P1, Pb1, work panel C over next 14 sts, Pb1, P1, Pb1, K1, work panel D over next 6 sts, K1, Pb1, P1, Pb1, work panel C over next 14 sts, Pb1, P1, Pb1, work panel A over last 36(40:44:48) sts.

Cont in this way, keeping pattern panels as set until work measures 26(26:28:28) cm from cast-on edge, or required length to underarm, ending with a wrong-side row.

Shape Armholes

Cast off 6(8:10:12) sts at beg of next 2 rows.

Dec 1 st at each end of next 6 rows.

Dec 1 st at each end of next and foll 3 alt rows.

Work without shaping, keeping patt correct until armholes measure 17(18:19:20) cm or 2 cm less than required length to shoulder, ending with a wrong-side row.

Shape Neck

1st row Patt 21(22:23:24) sts, P2 tog, turn.

Keeping patt correct dec 1 st at neck edge on foll 5 rows.

Shape Shoulder

Cast off 4 sts at beg of next and foll alt row.

Work 1 row.

Cast off 4(5:5:6) sts at beg of next row, patt to end.

Work 1 row.

Cast off rem 5(5:6:6) sts.

With right side of work facing slip centre 42(44:46:48) sts to holder for edging.

Rejoin yarn to rem sts.

1st row P2 tog, patt to end.

Dec 1 st at neck edge on foll 5 rows.

Work 1 row.

Shape Shoulder

Complete as for other shoulder.

Left Front

Using 3 mm needles cast on 52(56:60:64) sts.

1st row *Kb1, P1, rep from * to end.

2nd row *K1, Pb1, rep from * to end.

Rep 1st and 2nd rows 8 times more, then 1st row once.

Increase row Rib 11, M1, rib 9, M1, [rib 10, M1] 3 times, rib 2(6:10:14). 57(61:65:69) sts.

Change to 3¾ mm needles and begin pattern.

1st row Work panel A over next 36(40:44:48) sts, Kb1, P1, Kb1, work panel C over next 14 sts, [Kb1, P1] twice.

2nd row K1, Pb1, P1, Pb1, work panel C over next 14 sts, Pb1, P1, Pb1, work panel A over last 36(40:44:48) sts.

Cont in this way rep panel patts as required until work measures same as back to armhole, ending with a wrong-side row.

Shape Armhole

Cast off 6(8:10:12) sts, patt to end.

Work 1 row.

Dec 1 st at armhole edge on next 6 rows then on next and foll 3 alt rows.

Work 1 row.

Shape Neck

1st row Patt to last 16(17:18:19) sts, turn, leaving these sts on holder for neck edging.

Keeping patt correct dec 1 st at neck edge on next 5 rows, then on next and foll 2 alt rows. 17(18:19:20) sts.

Work without shaping until armhole measures same as back to shoulder, ending at armhole edge.

Shape Shoulder

Work as given for back.

Right Front

Using 3 mm needles cast on 52(56:60:64) sts.

1st row *P1, Kb1, rep from * to end.

2nd row *Pb1, K1, rep from * to end.

Rep 1st and 2nd rows 8 times more, then 1st row once.

Increase row Rib 2(6:10:14), [M1, rib 10] 3 times, M1, rib 9, M1, rib 11. 57(61:65:69) sts.

Change to 3¾ mm needles and begin pattern.

1st row [P1, Kb1] twice, work panel C over next 14 sts, Kb1, P1, Kb1, work panel B over last 36(40:44:48) sts.

2nd row Work panel B over next 36(40:44:48) sts, Pb1, P1, Pb1, work panel C over next 14 sts, Pb1, P1, Pb1, K1.

Cont in this way rep panel patts as required until work measures same as back to armhole ending with a right-side row.

Shape Armhole

Cast off 6(8:10:12) sts, patt to end.

Dec 1 st at armhole edge on next 6 rows then on next and foll 3 alt rows.

Work 1 row.

Complete to correspond with left front.

Button Band

Using 3 mm needles cast on 11 sts.

1st row P1, *Kb1, P1, rep from * to end.

2nd row K1, *Pb1, K1, rep from * to end.

Cont in rib in this way until band is required length from cast-on edge to centre front neck edge, ending with a wrong-side row.

Leave sts on holder.

Buttonhole Band

Mark position for 6 buttons on button band and work

buttonhole band in same way, casting off 3 sts in centre of band for each buttonhole as marker is reached. Cast on 3 sts on the foll row to replace those cast off. Leave sts on holder.

Neck Edging
Join both shoulder seams.

Using 3 mm needles and with right side of neck facing rib across 11 sts from buttonhole band thus, [P1, Kb1] 5 times, P tog last st and 1st st of front neck edge sts from holder, [Kb1, P1] 4 times, Kb1, P2 tog, [Kb1, P1] 2(2:3:3) times to last 0(1:0:1) st, Kb1, K up 52(54:56:58) sts along neck and shoulder edge to sts on holder at centre back, work across these sts thus – K 5(6:7:8), P2 tog, K 11, P2 tog, K 13, P2 tog, K 7(8:9:10), K up 52(54:56:58) sts to sts on front holder, rib 4(5:6:7), P2 tog, rib 9, P tog last st with 1st st of button band, rib to end.
Work 2 rows in twisted rib.
Cast off.

Armbands
Using 3 mm needles and with right side of armhole facing K up 97(99:101:103) sts. Work 2 rows of twisted rib. Cast off.

To Complete
Press each section lightly under a damp cloth with a warm iron, avoiding ribbing.

Join side seams. Sew front bands in place. Sew on buttons to correspond with buttonholes.

LACE STOLE FROM ESTONIA
This dainty cobweb lace stole contrasts the soft, solid bobbles of the branched pattern against the lighter background and is trimmed with a lace edging, added after knitting. (See colour plate 1.)

Materials
5 25 g balls of Templeton's H and O Shetland Lace
1 pair of 5 mm needles

Measurements
Approximately 47 cm wide and 122 cm long when complete.

Tension
1 pattern repeat of 15 sts measures 7.5 cm when blocked and pressed.

Special Abbreviations
MB make a bobble by working 7 sts into the next st in this way:

K into the next st putting the y2on, y2on, [K into same st putting y2on, y2on] twice, then K once more into same st putting y2on. On the next row these 7 sts are slipped, dropping the extra loop to make each st longer, and on the following row they are knitted tog, through the back of the loops.

SSK   sl next 2 sts to right needle singly and knitwise, insert tip of left needle through front of both slipped sts, from left to right, and K tog in this position.

Centre
Using 5 mm needles cast on 241 sts.
Preparation row K2, *SSK, K6, [yon, K1] twice, K2 tog, K1, yon, K2 tog, rep from *, ending last rep K2, in place of [K1, yon, K2 tog].
Next row P2, *P13, yon, P2 tog, rep from *, ending last rep P14.

Begin pattern
1st row K2, *SSK, K5, yon, K1, yon, MB in next st, K1, K2 tog, K1, yon, K2 tog, ending last rep K2, in place of [K1, yon, K2 tog].
2nd row P2, *P2, slip next 7 sts dropping extra yon from previous row on each loop, P10, yon, P2 tog, rep from *, ending last rep P11.
3rd row K2, *SSK, K4, yon, K1, yon, MB in next st, K1, K7 tog tbl, K2 tog, K1, yon, K2 tog, rep from *, ending last rep K2, in place of [K1, yon, K2 tog].
4th row P2, *P3, slip next 7 sts dropping extra loops, P9, yon, P2 tog, rep from *, ending last rep P10.
5th row K2, *SSK, K3, yon, K1, yon, MB in next st, K1, K7 tog tbl, K1, K2 tog, K1, yon, K2 tog, rep from *, ending last rep K2, in place of [K1, yon, K2 tog].
6th row P2, *P4, slip next 7 sts dropping extra loops, P8, yon, P2 tog, rep from *, ending last rep P9.
7th row K2, *SSK, K2, yon, K1, yon, MB, K1, K7 tog tbl, K2, K2 tog, K1, yon, K2 tog, rep from *, ending last rep K2, in place of [K1, yon, K2 tog].
8th row P2, *P5, slip next 7 sts dropping extra loops, P7, yon, P2 tog, rep from *, ending last rep P8.
9th row K2, *SSK, K1, yon, K1, yon, MB in next st, K1, K7 tog tbl, K3, K2 tog, K1, yon, K2 tog, rep from *, ending last rep K2, in place of [K1, yon, K2 tog].
10th row P2, *P6, slip next 7 sts dropping extra loops, P6, yon, P2 tog, rep from *, ending last rep P7.
11th row K2, *SSK, yon, K1, yon, MB in next st, K1, K7 tog tbl, K4, K2 tog, K1, yon, K2 tog, rep from *, ending last rep K2, in place of [K1, yon, K2 tog].
12th row P2, *P7, slip next 7 sts dropping extra loops, P5, yon, P2 tog, rep from *, ending last rep P6.

13th row K2, *SSK, K2, K7 tog tbl, K3, [yon, K1] twice, K2 tog, K1, yon, K2 tog, rep from *, ending last rep K2, in place of [K1, yon, K2 tog].

14th row P2, *P13, yon, P2 tog, rep from *, ending last rep P14.

Rep 1st–14th rows 6 times more, or for required length. Cast off.

Lace Edging

Using 5 mm needles cast on 11 sts.

Preparation row K9, yon, K2 (12 sts).

1st row K2, [K1, P1, K1] in yon of previous row, yon, P4 tog, K1, y2on, K2 tog, y2on, K2 (15 sts).

2nd row Sl 1, [K2, P1] twice, K2, [K1, P1, K1] in yon of previous row, yon, P4 tog, K1 (15 sts).

3rd row K2, [K1, P1, K1] in the yon of previous row, yon, P4 tog, K8 (15 sts).

4th row Cast off 3 sts, K5, [K1, P1, K1] in yon of previous row, yon, P4 tog, K1 (12 sts).

Rep 1st–4th rows until lace is required length to edge centre after pressing, allowing for fullness at corners. Cast off.

To Complete

Press centre after blocking, using a warm iron over a damp cloth. The surface will gain maximum light and shade if each bobble is gently raised with a blunt needle or fine knitting needle tip after pressing. Press lace edging also.

Pin the lace edge evenly round the centre and sew neatly in place, allowing extra fullness at each corner.

158 Detail of Estonian stole lace pattern

GLOVES FROM FAIR ISLE

The fine wool from Fair Isle is ideally suited to knitting gloves. Soft and pliable, it encases the fingers without uncomfortable bulk and makes for neat fitting wrists with the elasticity of one-and-one or two-and-two rib.

It is also exceedingly economical and a pair of gloves can be made from only two balls of the main shade, with small quantities of the colours used for the patterned bands on the hand.

Materials

2 25 g balls of Templeton's H and O Shetland Fleece
1 25 g ball, or small quantities of the same yarn in 5 colours
1 set of 4 double pointed needles, $2\frac{1}{4}$ mm

Tension

18 sts to 5 cm, measured over st st.

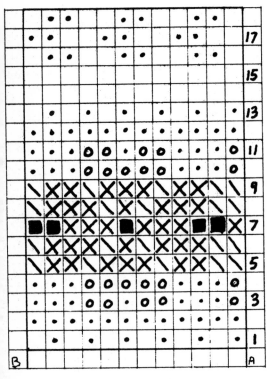

□ A Fawn or natural
· B Coral
o C Honey gold
\ D Peacock
× E White
■ F Sable

Fig. 113 Chart for Fairisle glove

Measurements
To fit average adult hand.
Finger and hand lengths are easily adapted to specific measurements.

Right Hand
**Using $2\frac{1}{4}$ mm needles and A, cast on 48 sts, and arrange on 3 needles each with 16 sts.
Work in rounds of K2, P2 rib until ribbing measures 7 cm.
Next round *K3, inc in next st, rep from * to end of round (60 sts).
Next round K.
Begin pattern.
Cont in st st, working from the chart.
Each round is worked from A to B and repeated to the end of the round.
Work rounds 1 to 18.**

Place Thumb
1st round Using A only, K1, slip next 10 sts onto holder or length of yarn for the thumb, turn, cast on 10 sts, turn and K to end of round.
***Next round* Using A, K (60sts)
Repeat rounds 1–13.
Divide for fingers.

First Finger
1st round K10, cast on 2 sts, sl next 44 sts onto holding thread, divide first 12 sts worked onto 2 needles and with 3rd needle K last 6 sts.
Work first finger on these 18 sts, using A only.
K 28 rounds or required finger length.
Shape top:
Next round *K2 tog, K1, rep from * to end.
Next round K.
Next round *K2 tog, rep from * to end.
Break off yarn, thread into wool needle and thread through rem sts.
Draw up and fasten off on wrong side.

Second Finger
1st round K up 2 sts from those cast on for 1st finger, K7 sts from those on holding thread, cast on 2 sts, K8 from the end of those on the holding thread. Divide these 19 sts onto 3 needles. K 32 rounds or required finger length.
Shape top:
Next round K1, *K2 tog, K1, rep from * to end.
Next round K.
Next round *K2 tog, rep from * to last st, K1.
Break off yarn and draw through rem sts. Finish off on wrong side.

Third Finger
1st round K up 2 sts from those cast on for 2nd finger, K7 sts from holding thread, cast on 2 sts, K7 from end of

holding thread. Divide these 18 sts onto 3 needles.
K 29 rounds or required finger length.
Work top as for 2nd finger.

Fourth Finger
1st round K up 2 sts from those cast on for 3rd finger, K rem 15 sts from holding thread. Divide these 17 sts onto 3 needles.
K 23 rounds or required finger length.
Work top as for third finger.

Thumb
1st round Using A, K across 10 sts from holder, K up 10 sts from those cast on for inner side of thumb. Divide these 20 sts onto 3 needles.
K 22 rounds or required thumb length.
Shape top:
Next round *K2 tog, rep from * to end.
Next round K.
Next round *K2 tog, rep from * to end.
Break off yarn, thread through rem sts and finish off on wrong side.

Left Hand
Work as for right hand from ** to **.

Place Thumb
1st round K to last 11 sts, cast on 10 sts, slip next 10 sts onto holder, K last st.
Complete as for other hand working from *** to end.

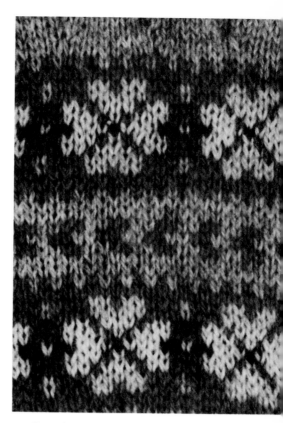

159 Detail of Fairisle pattern on gloves

SWEATER FROM GUERNSEY
Traditionally worked in navy wool this sweater is just as smart in dark green, grey or misty blues. (See colour plate 3.)

Materials
24(25:26:27) 25 g balls of Templeton's Ayrmist Double Knitting
1 set of 4 $3\frac{1}{4}$ mm needles pointed at both ends
1 circular $3\frac{1}{4}$ mm needle

Measurements
To fit an 85(90:95:100) cm chest.
Length to shoulder: 64(68:71:75) cm, or as required.
Sleeve length: 45(46:47:48) cm, or as required.

Tension
13 sts and 16 rows to 5 cm measured over st st worked on $3\frac{1}{4}$ mm needles.

Note
For a perfect finish use either of the cast-on methods, knotted edge or Guernsey edge (see *pages 61, 62*).

160 Detail of welt

Back
**Using 3¼ mm needle cast on 112(120:128:136) sts.
K 24 rows.**
Break yarn and leave on circular needle.

Front
Using circular needle work welt as for back from ** to **.

Back and Front
Join both welts into a circle by working across all sts as follows:
1st round *K1, P2, K1, rep from * to end of round.
Rep 1st round 5 times more.
Change to st st.
1st round K, inc 16 sts evenly on round.
240(256:272:288) sts.
2nd round *K120(128:136:144), M1 for seam st, rep from * once.
3rd round *K120(128:136:144), P1, rep from * once.
4th round K.
Rep last 2 rounds until work measures 39(41:43:45) cm, or approx 6 cm less than required length to underarm.

Divide for armholes
1st row *K120(128:136:144) sts, cast off 1 st, rep from * once.
Work front in rows:
1st row K6 including st rem from cast off st, P6, K to last 12 sts before cast-off seam st, P6, K6.
2nd row P.
Rep last 2 rows until armhole measures 25(27:28:30) cm, ending with a 2nd row.
Break yarn and leave sts on holder.

Back
With right side of work facing rejoin yarn to rem sts and work back as given for front.

To Complete Shoulders
Divide sts on both back and front into 3 groups of sts with 40(42:45:48) sts for each shoulder and 40(44:46:48) for neck. Place back and front together with wrong sides touching and cast off shoulders together taking 1 st from each side and knitting both sts tog, *K next st from front and back tog and lift over 1st st and off the needle, rep from * until 8 sts rem on both front and back shoulder.

Shoulder Gusset
1st row K next st on front needle, turn (2 sts).
2nd row P2, P 1 st from back needle, turn.
3rd row K3, K next st from front needle, turn.
4th row P4, P next st from back needle, turn.
Rep last 2 rows 6 times until all sts have been worked into gusset.

K across gusset sts and centre back to outer edge of other shoulder.

Work other shoulder and gusset in same way.

Neckband

Using set of 4 needles K up all rem sts from back and front neck and from both gussets, dec 1 st in centre of each gusset.

Work in rounds of K2, P2 rib for 3 cm.

Cast off in rib.

Sleeves

Using set of 4 needles cast on 64(64:68:68) sts.

Work in rounds of K2, P2 rib.

Work 7 cm.

Next round M1 for seam st, K to end of round inc 10 sts evenly.

2nd round P1, K to end.

3rd round K.

Rep last 2 rounds inc 1 st at each side of seam st on next and every foll 4th round until there are 115(119:123:127) sts.

Work without shaping until sleeve measures 37(38:39:40) cm or approx 8 cm less than required length.

Work Gusset

1st round M1, work seam st, M1, work to end of round.

Keeping seam st correct inc 1 st at either side on foll 8 alt rows.

Next round K9, work seam st, K9, P2, *K2, P2 rep from * to end.

Rep last round 5 times more.

Last round K9, work seam st, K9, cast off rem sts.

Complete gusset working in rows.

Keeping seam st as set dec 1 st at each side of seam st on next and every foll alt row until 3 sts rem.

Work 1 row.

Last row K3 tog, break off thread and draw through.

Work 2nd sleeve in same way.

To Complete

Using a grafted seam sew top of sleeves into armholes. Darn in all ends. Press garment, avoiding garter st and ribbing, using a warm iron over a damp cloth on the wrong side of the work.

161 Detail of armhole and front pattern

162 Norwegian sweater front detail

163 Detail of sleeve top

SWEATER FROM NORWAY

Worked in only two colours this traditional design is used in a slightly simplified form to make an outstanding sweater. The instructions are for the Norwegian method of working which is worth trying. Knitted completely round to the top of the armholes, the work is then cut for the insertion of the sleeves. Taken step by step, this presents no problem and makes for quicker and easier knitting as the pattern rounds are always facing and can be followed from the charts at a glance. (See colour plate 7.)

Materials

8(9:9:10) 50 g balls of Templeton's Norsk Ullgarn, main shade, A
3(3:4:4) balls of same yarn in contrast, B
1 set of $3\frac{1}{4}$ mm and $3\frac{3}{4}$ mm needles
1 circular needle in both $3\frac{1}{4}$ mm and $3\frac{3}{4}$ mm

Measurements

To fit an 85(90:95:100) cm bust/chest.
Length to shoulder: 61(62:64:65) cm or as required
Sleeve length: 44(44:46:48) cm or as required

Tension

24 sts and 32 rows to 10 cm measured over st st.

Sleeves

Using set of $3\frac{1}{4}$ mm needles and A, cast on 40(44:48:52) sts.
Work K2, P2 rib for 7 cm, inc 13(15:17:19) sts on last round.
Change to $3\frac{3}{4}$ mm needles and st st 53(59:65:71) sts.
1st round K up thread before 1st st and P into back of it, K to end of round. 54(60:66:72) sts.
Cont in st st, keeping 1st st P throughout as seam st and working pattern from chart A on K sts to left of P st.
Read from A1(A2:A3:A4) to B, work last st on chart (centre st) then work reading chart from B back to A1(A2:A3:A4).
K 2 rounds using A only, inc 1 st at each side of seam st on 1st round. 56(62:68:74) sts.
Place seeding pattern from chart B reading from A1(A2:A3:A4) to B, work centre st shown to left of B, then work from B back to A1(A2:A3:A4).
Work rows 1–4 then cont rep these rows inc 1 st at each side of seam st on every 3rd round, *at same time* working extra sts into seeding patt as they are made.
Work until there are 82(88:94:100) sts.
Work without shaping, keeping seeding patt correct, until sleeve measures 32(34:36:38) cm from cast-on edge or approx 10 cm less than required finished length, ending with a 4th patt round.

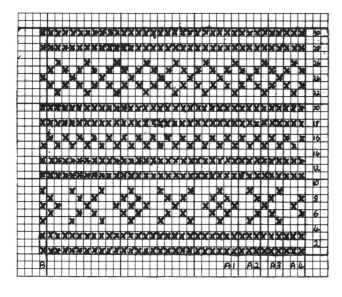

Fig. 114 Chart A, for Norwegian sweater

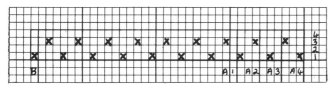

Fig. 115 Chart B

K 1 round using A only.
Work chart C reading from A1(A2:A3:A4) to B, work
centre st, then work from B back to A1(A2:A3:A4).
Place marker thread at end of last round.
K 4 rounds more using A only.
Cast off.
Work 2nd sleeve in same way.

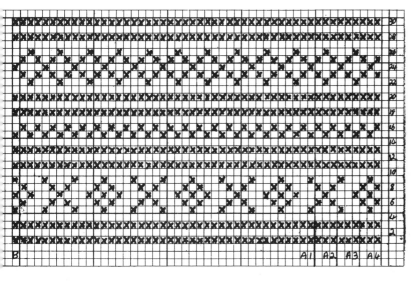

Fig. 116 Chart C

Body

Using circular $3\frac{1}{4}$ mm needle and A cast on 188(200:212:224) sts.

Work in K2, P2 rib for 5 cm, inc 18 sts evenly on last round.

Change to $3\frac{3}{4}$ mm circular needle and st st. 206(218:230:242) sts.

1st round Lift yarn before 1st st and P into back of it for 1st seam st, K103(109:115:121) sts, lift yarn before next st and P into the back of it for the 2nd seam st, K103(109:115:121) sts.

2nd round P1, place marker before next st, K103(109:115:121), place 2nd marker after last st, P1, place 3rd marker before next st, K103(109:115:121) place 4th marker after last st. The body pattern is worked between the 1st and 2nd markers for the front and between the 3rd and 4th markers for the back.

Work rounds 1–37 as shown on chart D, reading from A1(A2:A3:A4) to B, working centre st shown to left of B, then read from B back to A1(A2:A3:A4). Begin each round with a P st for the seam st working the pattern between the two sets of markers separated by the 2nd seam st.

The 37th round completes the 1st rep of the seeding patt. Rep 34th round to 37th round until work measures 42(43:45:46) cm or approx 19 cm less than required length to shoulder, ending with a 37th patt round.

Complete pattern band by working 38th–47th rounds then 5th–22nd rounds then 48th–57th rounds.

Divide for Neck

1st round Cast off 1st seam st, patt 58(62:66:70) sts as for 58th round on chart D, slip last 13(15:17:19) sts to holder for neck, patt to seam st, cast off 2nd seam st, patt across sts for back as for 58th round.

Complete Back

Working in rows complete chart D from 59th round to end. Leave sts on holder.

Right Front Neck

With wrong side of work facing rejoin yarn to 1st group of sts on front for right side. Keeping patt correct from chart dec 1 st at neck edge on next 7 rows then on next and alt rows 4 times in all. 34(36:38:40) sts. Complete last row from chart. Leave sts on holder.

Left front neck

With wrong side of front facing rejoin yarn to other shoulder and work to correspond, reversing shaping.

To Complete

Cast off shoulders together on wrong side, leaving centre 35(37:39:41) sts on holder for neckband.

Neckband

Using set of $3\frac{1}{4}$ mm needles and A and with right side of

164 Detail of lower border

Fig. 117 Chart D

neck facing K up 20 sts down side of neck K across
13(15:17:19) sts from front holder, K up 20 sts along other
side of neck and K 35(37:39:41) sts from centre back.
Work 20 rounds in K2, P2 rib.
Cast off loosely in rib.
Press under a damp cloth with a warm iron, omitting
ribbing.
Fold sleeves in half and mark depth required for armhole
(equal to half top sleeve width) down side seam. Stay

stitch around armhole 1 stitch in from edge. Cut down seam st to required depth. Fold back 3 sts around armhole and neaten cut edge with herringbone stitching. Lay top 4 rounds of sleeve over cut edge, sew in place around folded edge of armhole and on wrong side slip st cast-off edge over cut edge of body.
Press seams.

HANDKERCHIEF EDGING FROM SCOTLAND

This edging is similar to the lace surrounding the handkerchief knitted by Sarah McComb Rawson in California more than 100 years ago (*page 22*).

It can be worked in any fine yarn with suitable needles for the yarn used.

Lace Edging

Cast on 10 sts and K 1 row.
2nd row Sl 1, K1, [yon, K2 tog] twice, y4on, K2 tog, yon, P2 tog.
3rd row Yon, P2 tog, K1, [K1, P1] twice into loop made by y4on in previous row, [K1, P1] twice, K2.
4th row Sl 1, [K1, yon, K2 tog] twice, K4, yon, P2 tog.
5th row Yon, P2 tog, K5, [P1, K2] twice.
6th row Sl 1, K1, yon, K2 tog, K2, yon, K2 tog, K3, yon, P2 tog.
7th row Yon, P2 tog, K4, P1, K3, P1, K2.
8th row Sl 1, K1, yon, K2 tog, K3, yon, K2 tog, K2, yon, P2 tog.
9th row Yon, P2 tog, K3, P1, K4, P1, K2.
10th row Sl 1, K1, yon, K2 tog, K4, yon, K2 tog, K1, yon, P2 tog.
11th row Yon, P2 tog, K2, P1, K5, P1, K2.
12th row Sl 1, K1, yon, K2 tog, K5, yon, K2 tog, yon, P2 tog.
13th row Cast off 3 sts, slip the st from right-hand needle back to left needle, yon, P2 tog, K5, P1, K2.
Rep 2nd–13th rows until the lace is the required length to edge a handkerchief, allowing extra for easing round the corners.
Cast off.

To Complete

Starch the lace and pin out very evenly. Press and allow to dry completely before unpinning. Slip stitch or hem neatly around handkerchief edge.

LACE SCARF FROM SHETLAND

Plain or striped, this lace scarf uses the minimum amount of yarn possible for a scarf and makes the most of an incredibly simple lace stitch, consisting of only a two-row repeat.

165 Shetland lace scarf

Materials

For plain version:
2 25 g balls of Templeton's H and O Shetland Lace
For the striped version:
1 25 g ball of Templeton's H and O Shetland Lace in
background colour A (white), and 3 contrasting colours B,
C, and D (light, medium and dark)
For both versions:
1 pair of $4\frac{1}{2}$ mm needles

Tension

1 patte repeat of 11 sts measures 4 cm when blocked.

Measurements

26ccm wide and 100 cm long when blocked and finished.

Scarf

Using $4\frac{1}{2}$ mm needles and A, cast on 68 sts.
1st row K2, *yon, K3, K3 tog, K3, yon, K2, rep from * to
end.
2nd row K.
Rep these 2 rows until scarf is required length when
stretched or work in stripe sequence as follows: 14 rows A,
*4 rows B, 4 rows C, 2 rows A, 4 rows D, 2 rows B, 2 rows
A, 2 rows C, 2 rows A, 2 rows B, 4 rows D, 2 rows A, 4
rows C, 4 rows B, 12 rows A, **2 rows D, 2 rows A, 2 rows
C, 12 rows A. Rep from * once more then from * to **
once.
Complete to match other end by working 2 rows more
using A.
Cast off loosely. Darn in all ends.

Traditionally two scarves are dressed together by
catching the sides together through every row to form a
tube. This is thoroughly dampened then slipped onto a
smoothed shaped board and the end points are then
stitched together. The scarves are left to dry naturally
and are then separated and are ready for use.

   Where only one scarf is concerned it is best to block it
on a flat padded surface, drawing it out, after damping, to
its full size and pinning each row end and each point into
the pad. If possible leave to dry before removing pins. If it
is not possible to leave it then press it under a damp cloth
with a warm iron until completely dry. A light coating of
starch will keep the scarf looking its best and can be
added in spray form when pressing.

SHAWL FROM SHETLAND

Worked in natural colours or self-coloured, in pastels on
white or in the fashion colours of today, a shawl knitted
as it might have been over 100 years ago is still popular.
(See colour plate 2.)

166 Detail of lace scarf

Materials
Templeton's Shetland Fleece in main shade and 3 contrasts
11 25 g balls of main shade, A
2 25 g balls of 1st contrast, B
1 25 g ball of 2nd contrast, C
1 25 g ball of 3rd contrast, D
1 pair of 6½ mm needles

Measurements
Approx 160 cm square when complete.

Tension
16 sts and 22 rows to 10 cm measured over garter stitch, worked on 6½ mm needles.

Edging
Using a small length of contrast yarn cast on 9 sts.
The contrast yarn is removed when the edging is complete and is grafted to the other end to avoid the harshness of cast-on and cast-off edges.
Cont using A.
K 1 row.
1st row Yon, K2, yon, K1, K2 tog, yon, K4.
2nd row Yon, K2 tog, K2, K2 tog, yon, K2, yon, K1, K2 tog.
3rd row Yon, K2, yon, K3, K2 tog, yon, K4.
4th row Yon, K2 tog, K2, K2 tog, yon, K4, yon, K1, K2 tog.
5th row Yon, K2, yon, K5, K2 tog, yon, K4.
6th row Yon, K2 tog, K2, K2 tog, yon, K6, yon, K1, K2 tog.
7th row Yon, K2, yon, K7, K2 tog, yon, K4.
8th row Yon, K2 tog, K2, K2 tog, yon, K8, yon, K1, K2 tog.
9th row Yon, K2, yon, K9, K2 tog, yon, K4.
10th row Yon, K2 tog, K2, K2 tog, yon, K7, SK2togP, yon, K1, K2 tog.
11th row Yon, K2, yon, SK2togP, K6, K2 tog, yon, K4.
12th row Yon, K2 tog, K2, K2 tog, yon, K5, SK2togP, yon, K1, K2 tog.
13th row Yon, K2, yon, SK2togP, K4, K2 tog, yon, K4.
14th row Yon, K2 tog, K2, K2 tog, yon, K3, SK2togP, yon, K1, K2 tog.
15th row Yon, K2, yon, SK2togP, K2, K2 tog, yon, K4.
16th row Yon, K2 tog, K2, K2 tog, yon, K1, SK2togP, yon, K1, K2 tog.
17th row Yon, K2, yon, SK2togP, K2 tog, yon, K4.
18th row Yon, K2 tog, K2, K2 tog, yon, SKP, K1, K2 tog.
Rep 1st–18th rows 15 times more.
Do not break yarn but leave on holder for 2nd side.

First Side

With right side of edge facing and using A, K up 144 sts along the straight edge working 1 st into each loop made by the yon at the beginning of the row.

K 3 rows inc 1 st in centre of row on last row. (145 sts).

4th row Using B, [K2 tog] 8 times, *[yon, K1] 5 times, yon, [K2 tog] 3 times, K1, [K2 tog] 3 times, rep from * to last 21 sts, [yon, K1] 5 times, yon, [K2 tog] 8 times. (135 sts).

Using B, K 7 rows.

12th row Using C, [K2 tog] twice, K1, [K2 tog] 3 times, *[yon, K1] 5 times, yon, [K2 tog] 3 times, K1, [K2 tog] 3 times, rep from * to last 16 sts, [yon, K1] 5 times, yon, [K2 tog] 3 times, K1, [K2 tog] twice.

Using C, K 3 rows.

Using A, K 4 rows. (131 sts).

20th row Using D, K2 tog, K1, [K2 tog] 3 times, *[yon, K1] 5 times, yon, [K2 tog] 3 times, K1, [K2 tog] 3 times, rep from * to last 14 sts, [yon, K1] 5 times, yon, [K2 tog] 3 times, K1, K2 tog. (129 sts).

Using D, K 1 row.

Using C, K 6 rows. (129 sts).

28th row Using D, [K2 tog] 4 times, *[yon, K1] 5 times, yon, [K2 tog] 3 times, K1, [K2 tog] 3 times, rep from * to last 13 sts. [yon, K1] 5 times, yon, [K2 tog] 4 times. (127 sts).

Using D, K 1 row.

Using A, K 6 rows.

36th row Using B, [K2 tog] 4 times, [yon, K1] 4 times, yon, *[K2 tog] 3 times, K1, [K2 tog] 3 times, [yon, K1] 5 times, yon, rep from * to last 25 sts, [K2 tog] 3 times, K1, [K2 tog] 3 times, [yon, K1] 4 times, yon, [K2 tog] 4 times. (123 sts).

Using B, K 1 row.

Using C, K 6 rows.

44th row Using D, [K2 tog] twice, K3 tog, [yon, K1] 3 times, yon, *[K2 tog] 3 times, K1, [K2 tog] 3 times, [yon, K1] 5 times, yon, rep from * to last 23 sts, [K2 tog] 3 times, K1, [K2 tog] 3 times, [yon, K1] 3 times, yon, K3 tog, [K2 tog] twice. (117 sts).

Using D, K 1 row.

Using C, K 6 rows.

52nd row Using D, K2 tog, K3 tog, [yon, K1] twice, yon, *[K2 tog] 3 times, K1, [K2 tog] 3 times, [yon, K1] 5 times, yon, rep from * to last 20 sts, [K2 tog] 3 times, K1, [K2 tog] 3 times, [yon, K1] twice, yon, K3 tog, K2 tog. (111 sts).

Using D, K 3 rows.

Using C, K 4 rows.

60th row Using D, K3 tog, yon, K1, yon, *[K2 tog] 3 times, K1, [K2 tog] 3 times, [yon, K1] 5 times, yon, rep from * to last 17 sts, [K2 tog] 3 times, K1, [K2 tog] 3 times, yon, K1,

yon, K3 tog. (105 sts).
Using D, K 5 rows.
Using C, K 2 rows.
68th row Using D, K1, yon, *[K2 tog] 3 times, K1, [K2 tog] 3 times, [yon, K1] 5 times, yon, rep from * to last 14 sts, [K2 tog] 3 times, K1, [K2 tog] 3 times, yon, K1. (101 sts).
Using D, K 7 rows.
76th row Using A, K1, *K2 tog, yon, rep from * to last 2 sts, K2.
77th row K2, *K2 tog, yon, rep from * to last st, K1.
Cont on these sts using A only and working in garter stitch (every row knit) until the centre is square. Leave the sts on a holder to graft to the 3rd border.

Second Edging and Border

**Rejoin yarn to edging sts on holder and work 2nd edge and border as given for 1st edge and border working to 77th row of border.
K 1 row more.**
Graft the loops of this last row to the side of the centre square by working openwork row by threading needle with yarn, lifting 2 sts from row and 2 loops from edge onto needle, lifting 1st 2 over 2nd 2 and off needle tip; draw thread through rem 2, slip them off needle and rep to end of row.

Third Edging and Border

Work as for the second edging and border from ** to **. Graft this edge to the loops on holder for the centre square as for other edge.

Fourth Edging and Border

Work as for second edging and border from ** to ** and graft to rem side of square in same way.

To Complete

Remove the contrast coloured yarn from the cast-on edge and graft the last row of the edging to the first row.

Join the sides of the borders as invisibly as possible.

Thoroughly dampen the shawl and place it on a prepared flat surface on top of an unused bed or table that is covered with blanket or felt. Draw it out to its full size and pin it in place at each point so that the stitches are as uniform and the shape as perfect as possible. Leave until quite dry.

SWEATER FROM ICELAND

Soft, seamless and quick to knit, this sweater is not difficult to wear or to knit and its warmth and comfort make it a favourite in any wardrobe. (See colour plate 6.)

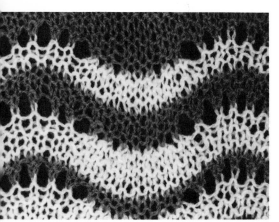

167 Detail of Shetland shawl border

Materials

Lopi Icelandic Yarn:
3(4:4:5) 100 g balls of main shade, A
1(1:1:1) 100 g ball of 1st contrast, B
1(1:1:1) 100 g ball of 2nd contrast, C
2 circular needles 5 mm (1 80 cm long and 1 40 cm long)
2 circular needles 6.5 mm (1 80 cm long and 1 40 cm long)

Measurements

To fit an 85(90:95:100) cm bust.
Length to shoulder: 60(62:64:66) cm, or as required.
Sleeve length: 43(44:45:46) cm, or as required.

Tension

14 sts and 20 rows to 10 cm measured over st st worked on
6.5 mm needle.

Sleeves

Begin at lower edge.
Using short 5 mm needle and B, cast on 28(30:32:34) sts.
Join into a circle, marking beg of round with a loop of
contrast coloured yarn.
Work in rounds of K1, P1 rib until cuff measures 6 cm.
Change to 6.5 mm short needle and st st.
1st round Using B, K inc evenly 12(10:16:14) times.
40(40:48:48) sts.
Work next 9 rounds from chart A, rep from A to B to end
of each round.
Using A only cont in st st.
Work 10 rounds.
Cont in st st, inc 1 st at each end of next and every 10th
round until there are 46(46:52:52) sts.
Work without shaping until sleeve measures
43(44:45:46) cm, or required sleeve length, ending
4(4:5:5) sts before end of last round.
Slip next 9(9:10:10) sts onto thread. Leave 37(37:42:42) sts
on needle.
Work 2nd sleeve in same way.

Body

Using long 5 mm needle and B, cast on
120(126:132:138) sts.
Work in rounds of K1, P1 rib for 6 cm, placing a contrast
marker at the start of the 1st round.
Change to long 6.5 mm needle and st st.
1st row Using B, K inc 8(10:12:14) times evenly in round.
128(136:144:152) sts.
Work next 9 rounds from chart A.
Using A only cont in st st until work measures

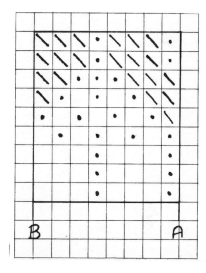

□ C Light
· B Dark
\ A Medium

*Fig. 118 Chart A for Icelandic
sweater*

168 Detail of Icelandic sweater at
lower edge

179

169 Yoke detail

Fig. 119 Chart B

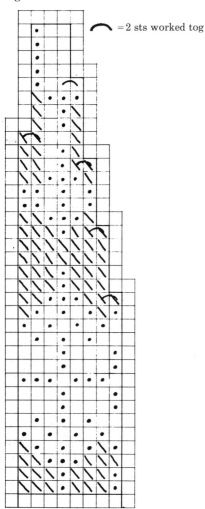

= 2 sts worked tog

37(39:41:43) cm from cast-on edge or required length to underarm, ending 4(4:5:5) sts before end of round.

Divide for Yoke

1st round Using A, K next 9(9:10:10) sts and leave on holder, K 55(59:62:66) sts for half body, K next 9(9:10:10) sts and leave on holder for 2nd armhole, K rem 55(59:62:66) sts.

Join for Yoke

1st round K across 37(37:42:42) sts from top of 1st sleeve, K across 55(59:62:66) sts from 1st half of body, K across 37(37:42:42) sts from 2nd sleeve top and K across rem 55(59:62:66) sts from 2nd half of body, leaving two groups of sts for underarm section on holders at either side. 184(192:208:216) sts.

Work rem rounds for yoke from chart B, rep from A to B to end of each round.

For 2nd, 3rd and 4th sizes only:

Rep last row of chart B 1(2:3) times.

Change to short 5 mm needle and A for neckband.

1st round K, dec 11 sts evenly in round.

Work in K1, P1 rib for 20 rounds.

Cast off loosely.

To Complete

Graft underarm stitches matching those on the sleeve top to those on the body.

Darn in all ends.

If required press lightly with a warm iron over a damp cloth on the wrong side of the work, avoiding ribbing sections.

MITTENS FROM LAPLAND

Decorated with a pattern worked in red and blue on a cream background, these mittens are easy and quick to knit and can be adapted for any size. The instructions are for a man's mitten but a change to a smaller needle size, 3 mm, giving 7 sts to 2.5 cm, will make the hand width more suitable for a woman.

Materials

2 25 g balls of Templeton's Ayrmist Double Knitting in main shade, A

Small quantities of the same yarn in 2 contrasting colours, B and C

1 set of 4 double pointed needles, $3\frac{1}{4}$ mm

Measurements

To fit an average adult hand.

Width around hand 20 cm.

Length from wrist 26 cm.

Tension

13 sts and 16 rows to 5 cm measured over st st.

Right Mitten

**Using 3¼ mm needles and B, cast on 54 sts.
Arrange sts on 3 needles.
1st round P1B, leave B hanging at front of work, join in
A, P1A, *leave A at front of work and lift B over it, P1B,
leave B at front and lift A over it, P1A, rep from * to end.
2nd round Using A, K.
3rd round Work as for 1st round using C in place of B.
4th round As 2nd round.
Rep last 4 rounds once then work 1st and 2nd rounds
once.
Cont using A only and working in st st.
Work 3 rounds.
Work pattern rounds 1–19 from chart A.
Cont using A only, K 8 rounds or required depth to base
of thumb.**

Place Thumb

1st round K1, slip next 11 sts onto length of yarn, cast on
11 sts, K to end.
***K 36 rounds or required length to start of top shaping.
Shape top:
1st round *K1, K2 tog tbl, K21, K2 tog, K1, rep from *
once.
2nd round *K1, K2 tog tbl, K19, K2 tog, K1, rep from *
once.
3rd round *K1, K2 tog tbl, K17, K2 tog, K1, rep from *
once.
4th round *K1, K2 tog tbl, K15, K2 tog, K1, rep from *
once.
5th round *K1, K2 tog tbl, K13, K2 tog, K1, rep from *
once.
6th round *K1, K2 tog tbl, K11, K2 tog, K1, rep from *
once.
7th round *K1, K2 tog tbl, K9, K2 tog, K1, rep from *
once.
8th round *K1, K2 tog tbl, K7, K2 tog, K1, rep from *
once.
9th round *K1, K2 tog tbl, K5, K2 tog, K1, rep from *
once.
10th round *K1, K2 tog tbl, K3, K2 tog, K1, rep from *
once.
11th round *K1, K2 tog tbl, K1, K2 tog, K1, rep from *
once.
12th round *K1, sl 1, K2 tog, psso, K1, rep from * once.
Break off thread and draw through rem sts, finishing off
on wrong side.

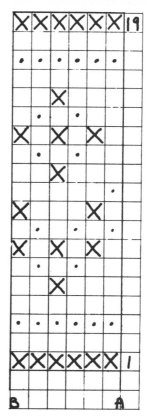

☐ White
· Red
× Blue

*Fig. 120 Chart A for
Lapp mittens*

170 Detail of Lapp mitten

181

171 Swedish cap

Fig. 121 Chart A for Swedish cap, chevron pattern for brim

□ White
· Red
∕ Blue
× Yellow

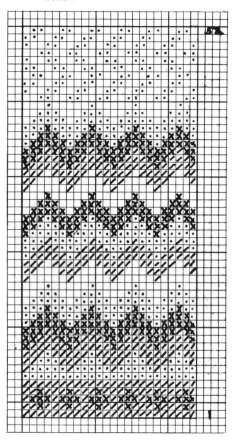

Thumb

Slip 11 sts from holding yarn onto needle, with right side facing K these 11 sts, K up 11 from cast-on edge at inner side of thumb. Arrange these 22 sts on 3 needles.
K 18 rounds or required depth of thumb to top shaping.
Shape top:
1st round *K1, K2 tog tbl, K5, K2 tog, K1, rep from * once.
2nd round *K1, K2 tog tbl, K3, K2 tog, K1, rep from * once.
3rd round *K1, K2 tog tbl, K1, K2 tog, K1, rep from * once.
4th round *K1, sl 1, K2 tog, psso, K1, rep from * once.
Break off yarn and thread through rem sts, finishing off on wrong side.

Left Mitten

Work as for right mitten from ** to **.

Place Thumb

1st round K to last 12 sts, slip next 11 sts onto holding yarn, cast on 11 sts, K1.
Complete as for right mitten from *** to end.

CAP FROM SWEDEN

Swedish caps are very varied and are often knitted completely double like a long tube shaped at each end. One half is folded inside the other, giving additional warmth and, because it is not seen, this half may be in plain yarn. The outer section may be patterned in many ways and also usually has a turn back brim which means four folds of material to keep ears warm in the coldest weather.

This cap is not double but is based on a traditional design worn by the famous Swedish fiddlers. A chevron pattern forms the brim while the main section is worked in a knitted version of an often used weaving pattern known as the goose-eye pattern.

Materials

1 50 g ball in each of 4 colours of Templeton's Norsk Ullgarn (original used white, blue, red and yellow)
1 set of $3\frac{1}{4}$ mm needles

Measurements

To fit an average adult head.

Tension

Approximately 12 sts and 15 rounds to 5 cm measured over patt.

Cap

Begin at brim edge
Using $3\frac{1}{4}$ mm needles and blue cast on 144 sts.
Work 4 rounds K1, P1 rib.

172 Detail of chevron pattern

Cont in st st.

Work from chart A from 1st–52nd round.

Turn work inside out to reverse for main section of head. With the wrong side of the work facing cont in st st beg with a K round.

Work main section from chart B working top shaping as indicated.

Break yarn leaving a 30 cm end. Thread end into wool needle and thread through rem sts. Seam to cast-on edge, reversing seam where knitting reverses.

Trim top with tassel of all colours, or two red pompons.

PATTERNED SOCKS FROM SCOTLAND

This traditional lace cable pattern is worn here by a young piper on her kilt hose but although attributed to Scotland, it is also a stitch pattern found in Austria and southern Germany. The socks are given in one size but are easily adapted for different leg lengths and foot lengths. The leg can be lengthened above the calf shaping or below it and the foot can be worked to any required length. Additional fitting is given by the elasticity of the ribbed panels between the openwork cable lines.

Materials

6 25 g balls of Templeton's Glenayr 4-ply
1 set of 3 mm double-pointed needles
1 cable needle

Measurements

Leg length with top folded to right side 28 cm or as required.
Foot length 21 cm or as required.

173 Detail of goose-eye pattern

Fig. 122 Chart B for goose-eye pattern

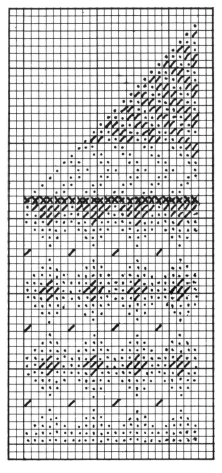

Tension
Equivalent to 15 sts to 5 cm measured over st st.

Special Abbreviation
C4 st next 2 sts to CN, hold at front, K next 2 sts tog, yon, K2 from CN.

Note The top scalloped turnover is worked with the wrong side facing so that it is correct when folded to the right side when the work is completed.

Sock
Using 3 mm needles cast on 120 sts, with 40 sts on each of 3 needles.

Join into a circle, taking care not to twist cast-on edge.

1st round *P1, yon, [P1, K1] 3 times, P1, P2 tog, K1, P2 tog tbl, P1, [K1, P1] 3 times, yon, rep from * to end.

2nd round *P1, yon, [K1, P1] 3 times, K1, P2 tog, P1, P2 tog tbl, K1, [P1, K1] 3 times, yon, rep from * to end.

Rep 1st and 2nd rounds 11 times more then 1st round once more, or until turnover is required depth.

Decrease round *P1, K3 tog, [P1, K1] twice, P2 tog, P1, P2 tog tbl, [K1, P1] twice, K3 tog, rep from * to end. (84 sts).

Next round *P1, K1, rep from * to end.

Rep last round 16 times more.

Next round *P1, K1, rep from * to last 6 sts, slip these 6 sts onto beg of 1st needle without working them in readiness for start of pattern which has central back cable lace panel at beg of 1st needle.

Preparation round *K1, K2 tog, yon, K2 tog tbl, P2, [K1, P1] twice, K1, P2, rep from * to end. (78 sts).

Begin pattern
1st round *K2 tog, yon, K2, P2, [K1, P1] twice, K1, P2, rep from * to end.

2nd round *K2, yon, K2 tog tbl, P2, [K1, P1] twice, K1, P2, rep from * to end.

3rd and 4th rounds As 1st and 2nd rounds.

5th and 6th rounds As 1st and 2nd rounds.

7th and 8th rounds As 1st and 2nd rounds.

9th round *C4, P2, [K1, P1] twice, K1, P2, rep from * to end.

10th round As 2nd round.

These 10 rounds form the lace cable pattern and are repeated throughout the leg and foot instep.

Cont in patt until leg measures 12 cm with top folded over or required length to start of leg shaping.

Next round Patt 4, P2 tog, patt to last 2 sts, P2 tog.

Keeping patt correct and noting that there are 2 sts less, 1 on each side of centre back cable panel, cont in patt for 9 rounds.

Dec 1 st at either side of back cable on next and every foll 10th round until 70 sts rem.

174 Kilt hose worn by a young piper patterned with a lace cable design

Cont without further shaping until leg measures 28 cm from top of turnover or required leg length to top of heel.

Divide for heel

1st row K20, slip last 16 sts of round onto other end of 1st needle to make 36 sts. Divide rem 34 sts onto 2 needles and leave until ready to work instep. The centre back cable should be in the centre of the 36 sts for heel.

1st row Sl 1 purlwise, P1, *sl 1 with yf, P1, rep from * to end.

2nd row Sl 1 knitwise, K to end.

Rep these 2 rows 15 times more then 1st row once more. To turn heel work as follows:

1st row K24, sl 1, K1, psso, turn.

2nd row P13, P2 tog, turn.

3rd row K13, sl 1, K1, psso, turn.

Rep 2nd and 3rd rows 9 times more, then 2nd row once.

Last row K7 to complete heel. Slip all 34 instep sts onto 1 needle.

Using spare needle K next 7 sts of heel and with same needle K up 17 sts along side of heel, using next needle patt across 34 instep sts, and with next needle K up 17 sts along other side of heel and K rem 7 sts from base of heel. (82 sts).

Shape instep

1st round 1st needle, K; 2nd needle, patt; 3rd needle, K.

2nd round 1st needle, K to last 3 sts, K 2 tog, K1; 2nd needle, patt; 3rd needle, K1, K2 tog tbl, K to end.

Rep last 2 rounds until 70 sts rem.

Keeping 1st and 3rd needles in st st and working patt on 2nd needle cont until work measures 12 cm from picked up sts at side of heel, or required foot length less approx 5 cm for toe shaping.

Shape toe

1st round 1st needle, K to last 4 sts, K3 tog, K1; 2nd needle, K1, K2 tog tbl, K to last 3 sts, K2 tog, K1; 3rd needle, K1, K3 tog tbl, K to end.

2nd round K.

3rd round 1st needle, K to last 3 sts, K2 tog, K1; 2nd needle, K1, K2 tog tbl, K to last 3 sts, K2 tog, K1; 3rd needle, K1, K2 tog tbl, K to end.

Rep 2nd and 3rd rounds until 28 sts rem.

To complete, using the 3rd needle just worked knit across the sts from the 1st needle.

Place both needles together and graft the stitches or cast off both needles together.

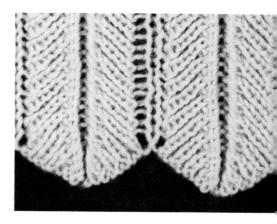

175 Detail of sock turnover

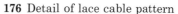

176 Detail of lace cable pattern

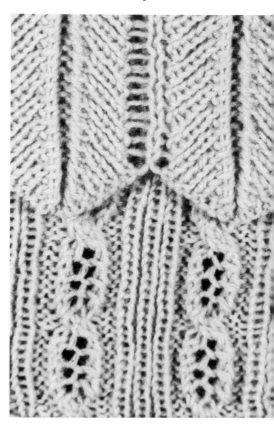

SUPPLIERS

U.K.

James Templeton and Son Ltd
Mill Street
Ayr
KA7 1TL
Scotland
*In case of difficulty in obtaining H. and O.
Shetland Fleece, H. and O. Shetland Lace,
Norsk Ullgarn or Ayrmist Double Knitting,
the above will supply the address of the
nearest stockist, or make arrangements for the
purchase of the required yarn.*

Scotnord Ltd
Crieff
Perthshire
Scotland
Lopi Icelandic yarns

Stove and Smith
98 Commercial Street
Lerwick
Shetland
*Steel double-pointed needles for Fairisle
knitting*

Goodlad and Goodlad
90 Commercial Street
Lerwick
Shetland
Leather knitting belts

U.S.A.

The Wool Shop
250 Birch Hill Road
Locust Valley, N.Y.
Templeton's Aran 100% Wool

The Little Mermaid
At the Castle
205 E. Lawrence St
Appleton, Wis. 54911

The Woolgatherer Inc.
1502 Twenty-First Street, N.W.
Washington D.C. 20036
*Templeton's H. and O. Shetland lace and H.
and O. Shetland fleece*

Reynolds Yarns Inc., Hauppauge,
N.Y. 11787
Lopi Icelandic yarn

In addition all Templeton's yarns are
available direct through their complete mail
order service from:
James Templeton and Son Ltd
Mill Street
Ayr
KA7 1TL
Scotland.

NEEDLE SIZE CHART

Metric	English before metrication	American
2	14	00
$2\frac{1}{4}$	13	0
$2\frac{1}{2}$		1
$2\frac{3}{4}$	12	1
3	11	2
$3\frac{1}{4}$	10	3
$3\frac{1}{2}$		
$3\frac{3}{4}$	9	4
4	8	5
$4\frac{1}{2}$	7	6
5	6	7
$5\frac{1}{2}$	5	8
6	4	9
$6\frac{1}{2}$	3	10
7	2	$10\frac{1}{2}$
$7\frac{1}{2}$	1	11
8	0	12
9	00	13
10	000	15

METRIC CONVERSION CHART

cm	in
0.5	$\frac{3}{16}$
1	$\frac{3}{8}$
2	$\frac{3}{4}$
3	$1\frac{1}{8}$
4	$1\frac{5}{8}$
5	2
6	$2\frac{3}{8}$
7	$2\frac{3}{4}$
8	$3\frac{1}{8}$
9	$3\frac{1}{2}$
10	4
20	$7\frac{7}{8}$
30	$11\frac{7}{8}$
40	$15\frac{3}{4}$
50	$19\frac{5}{8}$
100	$39\frac{3}{8}$

GLOSSARY OF ENGLISH AND AMERICAN TERMS

English	American
Cable needle (CN)	Double-pointed needle (dpn)
Cast off	Bind off
Double crochet (dc)	Single crochet
Treble	Double crochet
Double treble	Treble
Stocking stitch	Stockinette
Tension	Gauge

CONVERSION CHART FOR BALL WEIGHTS

Balls vary in size and may be marked in ounces or grams.
This chart shows the number of 20g, 25g and 50g balls
required when the original amount is shown in ounces.

oz	20g	25g	50g	oz	20g	25g	50g
1	2	2	1	13	19	15	8
2	3	3	2	14	20	16	8
3	5	4	2	15	22	17	9
4	6	5	3	16	23	19	10
5	8	6	3	17	25	20	10
6	9	7	4	18	26	21	11
7	10	8	4	19	27	22	11
8	12	10	5	20	29	23	12
9	13	11	6	21	30	24	12
10	15	12	6	22	32	25	13
11	16	13	7	23	33	27	14
12	17	14	7	24	34	28	14

BIBLIOGRAPHY

BALNEAVES E., *The Windswept Isles*, John Gifford, London, 1977.

BIRD B., *Paracas Fabrics and Nazca Needlework*, New York, 1974.

BØHN A.S., *Norwegian Knitting Designs*, Grøndahl and Søn, Oslo, 1952.

BRAND J., *A Brief Description of Orkney, etc.*, 1701.

BRIDGEMAN H. and DRURY E., *Illustrated History of Needlework*, Paddington Press, London, 1978.

BUHLER-OPPENHEIM K., *Die Textilien Sammlung Fritz Iklé-Huber*, Zurich, 1948.

COMPTON R., *Practical Knitting*, Hamlyn, London, 1981.

COMPTON R. and HARVEY M., *Fisherman Knitting*, Shire Publications, Aylesbury, 1978.

DEBES H.M., *Føroysk Bindingarmynstur, Føroyskt Heimavirki*, Tørshavn, 1969.

d'HARCOURT R., *Ancient Textiles of Peru and Their Techniques*, University of Washington, 1974.

DILLMONT T. de, *Encyclopedia of Needlework*, Dolfus Mieg and Co., Mulhouse, 1896.

DUBUISSON M., *La Bonneterie au Moyen-age*, Needlework and Bobbin Club 52, 1969.

FANDERL L., BAUERLICHES STRICKEN, 1, Rosenheimer, Rosenheim, 1975.

FANDERL L., BAUERLICHES STRICKEN, 2, Rosenheimer, Rosenheim, 1979.

FENTON A., *The Northern Isles: Orkney and Shetland*, J. Donald, Edinburgh, 1978.

FORIS M. and A., *History of Folk Cross Stitch*, Sebaldus, Nuremberg, 1960.

GAUGAIN J., *The Lady's Assistant*, vol. 1 and 11, I. J. Gaugain, Edinburgh, 1844.

GAUGAIN J., *The Accompaniment to the Second Volume of Mrs Gaugain's Work*, I. J. Gaugain, Edinburgh 1844.

GAUGAIN J., *The Knitter's Friend*, I. J. Gaugain, Edinburgh, 1846.

GERAMB B., *Steirisches Trachtenbuch*, vol. 1 and 11, Graz, 1932.

GRASS M. and A., *Stockings for a Queen*, Heinemann, London 1967.

GUÐJÓNSSON E.E., *Notes on Knitting in Iceland*, National Museum of Iceland, Reykjavik, Iceland, 1979.

HAGLUND U. and MESTERTON I., *Bohus Stickning*, Atlantis, Goteborg, 1980.

HARLOW E., *The Art of Knitting*, Collins, Glasgow and London, 1977.

HARTLEY M. and INGILBY J., *The Old Handknitters of the Dales*, The Dalesman Publishing Co., Ltd, Clapham, N. Yorks., 1951.

JOHANSSON B. and NILSSON K., *Binge – en Hallandsk Sticktradition*, Helsingborg, 1980.

LAMBERT A., *My Knitting Book*, John Murray, London, 1844.

LARSSON M., *Stickat fran Norbotten*, A.B. Boktryck, Helsingborg, 1978.

LEANDER C., *Kunst Strickerei*, Hennings und Hopf, Erfurt, 1848.

LEANDER C., *Kunst Strickerei*, Hennings und Hopf, Erfurt, 1852.

NETTO T.F., *Die Kunst Zu Stricken*, Leipzig, 1800.

NORBURY J., *Traditional Knitting Patterns*, Batsford, London, 1962.

NYLÉN A-M., *Stickning*, Hemslöjd, Lund, 1969.

OLKI M., *Kirjokintaita werner söderström osakeyhtiö*, Porvoo, Helsinki, 1953.

PHILIPS M.W., *Step By Step Knitting*, Golden Press, New York, 1967.

PLOUG M., *Strikkede Nattrøjer På Danske Museer*, Danmarks Folkelige Broderier, Arhus, 1979.

POSTLETHWAITE M., *Universal Dictionary of Trades*, Aberdeen, 1774.

Textile History, vols, 1, 2, 4 and 7, The Pasold Research Fund Ltd, Edington, Wilts.

RIEGLIN D.D., *Neus und Zum Stricken*, W. Thail, Nuremburg, 1760.

SCHMEDDING B., *Mittelalterliche Textilien in Kirchen und Klöstern der Schweiz*, Inverlag Stampfli and Cie A.G., Berne.

SCHMID A., *Allerhard Model zum Stricken*, 1748.

SCHNEIDER J., *Textilien*, National Swiss Museum, Zurich, 1975.

SCHWER I., *Stricken Heuse*, Leopold Stocker, Graz, 1969.

STEFFENSEN H., *Nålebinding*, Borgens Forlag, Odense, 1975.

SMITH M. and TWATT N., *A Shetland Pattern Book*, The Shetland Times Ltd, Lerwick, 1979.

SNOWDEN J., *The Folk Dress of Europe*, Mills and Boon Ltd, London, 1979.

THOMAS M., *Mary Thomas's Knitting Book*, Hodder and Stoughton, London, 1938.

THOMAS M., *Mary Thomas's Book of Knitting Patterns*, Hodder and Stoughton, London, 1948.

THOMPSON G., *Guernsey and Jersey Patterns*, Batsford, London, 1955.

TROTZIG E., *Stickning, Tradition och Kultur*, LTs Förlag, Stockholm, 1980.

TURNAU I., *Historia Dziewiarstwa Europejskiego do Poezatke XIX Wiekie*, Polskie Academia Nauk, Instytiet Historia Kultury. Materialneg (Ossolineum) Warsaw, 1979.

UTTLEY J., *The Story of the Channel Islands*, Faber and Faber, London, 1966.

WINTZELL I., *Sticka Mönster*, Nordiska Museet, Stockholm, 1976.

WINTZELL I., *Sticka med Hemslöjden*, LTs Förlag, Stockholm, 1979.

INDEX